ARTISTS OF THE HARLEM RENAISSANCE

DUKE ELLINGTON

MUSICIAN

REBECCA CAREY ROHAN

Cavendish
Square

New York

Published in 2017 by Cavendish Square Publishing, LLC
243 5th Avenue, Suite 136, New York, NY 10016

First Edition

Website: cavendishsq.com

This publication represents the opinions and views of the author based on his or her personal
experience, knowledge, and research. The information in this book serves as a general guide only.
The author and publisher have used their best efforts in preparing this book and disclaim liability
rising directly or indirectly from the use and application of this book.

CPSIA Compliance Information: Batch #CS16CSQ

All websites were available and accurate when this book was sent to press.

Library of Congress Cataloging-in-Publication Data

Names: Rohan, Rebecca Carey, 1967- author.
Title: Duke Ellington : musician / Rebecca Carey Rohan.
Description: New York : Cavendish Square Publishing, 2017. |
Series: Artists of the Harlem Renaissance | Includes bibliographical references and index.
Identifiers: LCCN 2015035470 | ISBN 9781502610607 (library bound) |
ISBN 9781502610614 (ebook)
Subjects: LCSH: Ellington, Duke, 1899-1974. | Jazz musicians–United
States–Biography.
Classification: LCC ML410.E44 R64 2016 | DDC 781.65092–dc23
LC record available at http://lccn.loc.gov/2015035470

Editorial Director: David McNamara
Editor: Elizabeth Schmermund
Copy Editor: Nathan Heidelberger
Art Director: Jeffrey Talbot
Designer: Stephanie Flecha
Senior Production Manager: Jennifer Ryder-Talbot
Production Editor: Renni Johnson
Photo Research: J8 Media

The photographs in this book are used by permission and through the courtesy of:

Gjon Mili/The LIFE Picture Collection/Getty Images, cover; Keystone-France/Gamma-Keystone via Getty Images,
back cover; Franz Hubmann/Imagno/Getty Images, 5; Thomas D. Mcavoy/The LIFE Picture Collection/Getty
Images, 6; Library of Congress, 12-13, PF(bygone1)/Alamy Reportage Archival†image, 16; Henry P. Whitehead
Collection/Anacostia Community Museum, 18; Schomburg Center for Research in Black Culture, Photographs
and Prints Division/ Regina Andrews photograph collection/NYPL, 20; Duke Ellington Collection, Archives Center,
National Museum of American History/SIRIS, 22, 62, 98-99; Jamees Kriegsmann/Michael Ochs Archives/Getty
Images, 24; Gilles Petard/Redferns, 28; Eliot Elisofon/The LIFE Picture Collection/Getty Images, 31; Bridgeman
Images, 33; Michael Ochs Archives/Getty Images, 37; Paul Hoeffler/Redferns, 38-39; Fulton-Larson Company,
Chicago/ File:Great Northern pullman car in day mode 1926.JPG/Wikimedia Commons, 42; Daniel Dempster
Photography Alamy, 44; Smithsonian Institution, 47; Everett Collection Historical Alamy, 50; Album/Newscom, 52,
69; Pictorial Press Ltd/Alamy, 56; AP Photo, 58; National Archives/File:Richard M. Nixon presenting the Presidential
Medal of Freedom to Duke Ellington. - NARA - 194289.tif/Wikimedia Commons, 61; Michael Ochs Archives/
Getty Images, 65; Gilles Petard/Redferns, 74; Walter McBride/Wirelmage, 76; PhotoQuest/Getty Images, 78;
OldMagazineArticles.com, 83; Bill Wagg/Redferns/Getty Images, 85; Charles 'Teenie' Harris/Carnegie Museum
of Art/Getty Images, 87; AP Photo/John Lent, 91; Everett Collection Historical Alamy, 94; Don Emmert/AFP/Getty
Images, 96; Jack Mitchell/Getty Images, 103; Jack Vartoogian/Getty Images, 107; Michael Ochs Archives/Getty
Images, 109; Citizen of the Planet/Alamy, 111; Walter McBride/Wirelmage, 113.

Printed in the United States of America

TABLE OF CONTENTS

PART 1

The Life of Duke Ellington

"Music is how I live, why I live and how I will be remembered."

—Duke Ellington's last words, May 24, 1974

Opposite: Duke Ellington spent much of his five-decade career sitting at the piano, whether composing or performing.

CHAPTER ONE

IN THE BEGINNING

omposer. Bandleader. Songwriter. Musician. Edward "Duke" Ellington was all of those things, yet he accomplished so much more. While he started his career as a pianist, he became the leader of a jazz orchestra—the only major leader of a jazz orchestra who also composed most of the music he played. He was instrumental in spreading the popularity of the ragtime sound and jazz music, yet he refused to call himself a jazz musician. He called his work Negro music, American music, or "the music of my people."

And he was right: jazz, as an art form, was invented by Americans. It originated in New Orleans, Louisiana, a city with a distinct culture that was a melting pot of African Americans, Native Americans, and families of European descent. Jazz music sprang from the musical traditions of both Africa and Europe. Duke Ellington took those traditions and made them his own.

Opposite: The police enforced segregation of whites and African Americans at this concert at the Lincoln Memorial.

Yet, his rise to fame is not the stereotypical rags to riches story, nor was his genius discovered at an early age. Edward Kennedy Ellington was born in Washington, DC, in 1899, into a stable, loving family. He was the first child of Daisy and James Ellington, and also their only child for the first sixteen years of his life, until his sister Ruth was born in 1915. He would be the first to admit that he was a spoiled, **coddled** child who was raised to feel that he was special.

His mother, Daisy Kennedy Ellington, was not only a beauty; she was an educated woman. She had completed high school, which was rare for a black woman at that time. Her father was a policeman who knew many important Washingtonians. She supposedly had a white grandfather and a Native American grandmother. Daisy taught her son Edward spirituality and discipline.

His father, James Edward Ellington, worked for a time as a butler and house manager for a well-known white physician, and he occasionally worked catering jobs at the White House. He taught his son how to be a refined young gentleman, based on what he had observed on the job. He was also outgoing, witty, and a practiced flirt—traits he passed on to his son.

At the time of Edward's birth, Washington, DC, was a **segregated** city. African-American and white people went to different schools, sat in different sections of restaurants and theaters, and did not mix socially. Even at the dedication of the Lincoln Memorial, a symbol of equality, African Americans had to sit in a segregated area. The newspapers run by whites rarely published stories about the positive achievements of African Americans, but they were only too happy to print stories about crimes in black neighborhoods—whether they were true or not.

Edward, however, was raised in the Northwest section of the District of Columbia, an **enclave** of ambitious African Americans, many of whom had moved there from the South to have a better chance at making a living. James Ellington was one of them. He had moved to the District from North Carolina, and he eventually worked his way up the social scale from being a butler to becoming a blueprint maker for the US Navy.

Especially due to opportunities in government employment, Washington, DC, had a large African-American **middle class** at the time. It was also one of the few cities in America where African Americans owned stores or other businesses, practiced medicine or dentistry, or worked as teachers. The schools may have been segregated, but they were good schools. At the turn of the century, Washington had the largest black population in the country, more so than even New Orleans, Philadelphia, or New York City. It was a place of promise for many people of color, and the community as a whole inspired its citizens to aim high. Edward's family shared those values and ambitions with their son.

Perhaps most importantly for aspiring musicians, Washington offered a wide variety of musical experiences. Edward's community offered choral ensembles, musical theater, and concert artists. There were plenty of bands, and dance halls for them to play in. Music was everywhere in the city. Duke Ellington once said, "Washington was a very good climate for me to come up in musically."

James and Daisy Ellington were solidly middle class, with enough money to afford comfortable row-house apartment homes, to insist on good manners and proper coat-and-tie dress, and to enjoy the elegant food and wine that James sometimes brought home from catering jobs. They spent summers at the seashore. Most importantly, they had the means to own an upright piano.

Edward went to black schools and black churches—in fact, he went to church twice every Sunday, once to his father's church and once to his mother's. Even though his parents embraced different religions, Edward's sister Ruth described their household as a "house full of love." The house was also full of music: both of his parents played the piano, and his father sang in a barbershop quartet. Edward himself began taking piano lessons when he was only six years old. He seemed to have a passion and talent for playing popular music, but like many young children, he got bored with playing scales and drills. For several years, he turned his attention to sports, especially baseball.

YEARS OF CHANGE

By the time he was in middle school, Edward had stopped taking piano lessons altogether. He had discovered that he had a talent for drawing and painting and wanted to explore the possibilities that such a talent could provide. In fact, he went into high school planning to pursue commercial art.

While a student at Armstrong High School, Edward entered and won a poster contest sponsored by the National Association for the Advancement of Colored People (NAACP). The prize was a scholarship to study at the Pratt Institute, a college of art and design in Brooklyn, New York.

Fortunately for the world, Edward also began sneaking into Washington clubs and performance halls around this time. He was drawn to the music of the ragtime musicians and stride piano masters that he had grown up enjoying, and he wanted to create music again. He decided to turn down the Pratt Institute and devote his time to his first love: music, and specifically the piano. The rest became history.

Nobody knows exactly when Edward Ellington picked up the nickname of "Duke," but it happened early in his life, probably during his teen years. Even as a teenager, he dressed well and always had good manners. Some say he gained his nickname from his "duked up" appearance, while others say he earned it for his gentlemanly ways.

What everybody does know is that Duke Ellington wrote his first piece, "Soda Fountain Rag," at the age of seventeen, inspired by his job working at—of course—a soda fountain, called the Poodle Dog Cafe. A rag is a song that's played in the ragtime style, which became popular at the turn of the century. The beat in ragtime isn't smooth. It's ragged, which is where the term "ragtime" comes from. Ellington later said he wrote the song based on the rhythms of the machine that he used to squirt carbonated water into the sodas he made. He followed a similar path to composing throughout his career, turning things he saw and heard into the basis for songs.

Ellington also said that he had no choice but to compose his own pieces when he was younger because he lacked formal training and couldn't read music. That didn't stop him from being a popular performer when he was still in high school. He began playing piano at senior dances and soon his services were in demand for teenage parties and other get-togethers. He worked hard to improve his piano playing and performance style, and he studied another pianist named James P. Johnson, who specialized in a style called Harlem Stride. Little did Ellington know that he would soon meet Johnson and receive encouragement from him.

Ellington's renewed commitment to music occurred at the perfect time. In the early 1900s, dancing in public was becoming more acceptable. By 1916, when Ellington was seventeen, multiple dance halls had opened in Washington to accommodate this new trend. Hanging around the clubs and halls, he met and learned from many working musicians, both local and national. One special mentor was Washington bandleader Oliver "Doc" Perry, who taught Ellington elements of music theory and how to read music. Perry also showed Ellington that it was important to develop a professional attitude toward performing.

Armstrong Technical High School, where Edward "Duke" Ellington studied design and art. Armstrong was one of only two public high schools for black students in Washington, DC.

IMAGE WAS EVERYTHING

While nobody knows exactly how and when Duke Ellington acquired his nickname, it stuck because it fit his image. His parents had raised him with careful manners. His teachers had impressed upon him the importance of speaking correctly and presenting a successful image to the world. "He was a self-educated man, but if you heard him speak, you thought he had attended the finest university in the world," said June Norton, a vocalist with the Ellington orchestra

Duke loved the finer things in life, especially new clothes. Rex Stewart, who played cornet for eleven years in the Duke Ellington Orchestra, once said, "To all the style-conscious musicians, Duke was considered the epitome of elegance."

At one point in his life, Duke supposedly owned 150 suits and 1,000 ties. In the 1930s, he traveled with five trunks of clothes plus a separate trunk for shoes. He wore expensive cashmere sweaters to rehearsal. His shoes, hats, shirts, and cologne were custom-made. In photographs, Duke always appeared impeccably dressed from head to toe in coordinated hats, suits, and ties, with a well-groomed mustache and carefully styled hair. As a bandleader, he always wore a tuxedo.

Another of Ellington's teachers was Henry Grant, the music supervisor in the local school system, who lived down the street from James and Daisy's house. Grant was a versatile and well-connected musician. He composed, directed more than one church choir, led a glee club, and played piano in a performing trio. Grant taught Ellington elementary harmony twice a week. He also let Ellington know that there was nothing wrong with popular music, which most trained musicians looked down on.

As his knowledge expanded and his skills improved, Ellington began filling in for Perry and other musicians in African-American clubs and cafes all over Washington. Perry taught Ellington more than just how to read music. He had an influence on his student's outward appearance as well. Ellington once described Perry this way: "He was intelligent, had a beautiful posture at all times—sitting, walking in a poolroom, or playing the piano—and talked with a semi-continental finesse. He was extremely dignified, clean, neat, and had impeccably manicured nails and hands. While playing the piano, he had the form that athletes have ... Doc Perry was an impressive sight no matter what he was doing." Ellington could easily have been describing himself.

Around the same time, Ellington met Louis Brown, another trained musician who was active in concerts, clubs, theaters, and church choirs in Washington, DC. He was also a tall, charismatic bandleader with a distinctive technique and an ability to play in a wide variety of styles—like Ellington himself. Brown and Perry, whether directly or indirectly, became mentors to Duke Ellington and showed him the value of being a gracious entertainer and a well-rounded musician.

In 1917, at the age of eighteen, Duke Ellington joined his first band, along with his friend Otto "Toby" Hardwick, drummer Sonny Greer, banjo player Elmer Snowden, and trumpeter Arthur Whetsol.

James P. Johnson, one the best-known practitioners of the Harlem Stride

Known as either Duke's Serenaders or The Duke's Serenaders, the band performed at dance halls throughout the Washington, DC, area. Most of the band members, except Sonny Greer, were still in their teens. In fact, Arthur Whetsol was only twelve years old. The lineup for the Serenaders would change from night to night, depending on whether or not the boys' parents would let them leave the house at night to perform!

Because these boys all came from similar backgrounds, they shared certain characteristics: they all had a respect for education, for the art of music, for order, and for conducting themselves professionally. These qualities would serve them well throughout their career.

The Serenaders played their first **gig** at the True Reformers Hall, which still stands on U Street in Washington, DC. Back then, U Street was at the heart of a lively area known as "Black Broadway" because of its many music clubs, theaters, and restaurants and its location in the heart of the country's largest urban, African-American community. The night was a success: Ellington made seventy-five cents for five hours of work, which was a good amount of money at the time.

One way the Serenaders got their bookings was through Ellington's other job; he had started a sign-painting business to support himself while launching his musical career. If a customer asked him to create an advertisement for a dance, he would ask if the dance needed a band. When someone wanted to hire a band for a dance, he would ask if the dance needed a sign painter.

Indeed, Ellington had discovered that he had a head for business. Once, another pianist had asked him to play a gig. That pianist paid him $10 out of the $100 fee the engagement paid. Ellington realized that managing a band could be **lucrative**, so he became a booking agent himself. He often managed as many as five bands a night.

One of Duke Ellington's advertisements for the irresistible "jass" provided by the Serenaders

Between Ellington's skill for advertising and his personality and showmanship, by March 1918, the Serenaders were getting jobs outside the black community, at embassies, private mansions, and Virginia society balls. Ellington was able to move out of his parents' home and pay for a telephone—which was a luxury back then. It was an important luxury, though, because he had listed himself in the yellow pages of the telephone book as a musician, and he needed to be able to take booking calls.

Ellington also picked up a few tricks, like always speaking quickly when potential customers called so he would sound busy. When he realized that other bands were placing larger ads in the telephone book than his ads, he decided that he had to compete with them. He placed an ad in the yellow pages that was as large as the ads for the other bands, and sure enough, he started getting more calls about gigs. He understood early on that being a good businessman was almost as important as being a good musician!

A CULTURAL EXPLOSION

As Ellington was making a name for himself in Washington, DC, the Harlem Renaissance was about to take off in New York City. At the time, Harlem was a large, primarily African-American neighborhood in Manhattan, much like the area of Washington, DC, where Elligton had grown up. It had become a cultural and intellectual center for African Americans after the Great Migration of Southern blacks to Northern cities in the early 1900s. This triggered a period of tremendous cultural and artistic growth in the African-American community, lasting from approximately 1918 to 1937.

In fact, the Harlem Renaissance has been described as "an explosion of arts and literature." It was a relatively short but intense period of time during which many African-American writers, artists, musicians, and **activists** worked to support and promote black heritage and culture in American life. Writers like Langston Hughes and Zora Neale Hurston, actor Paul Robeson, and activists W. E. B. Du Bois (who started the NAACP) and Marcus Garvey gained fame and attention. It was also during this period that the great Harlem jazz clubs opened, such as the Cotton Club, the Savoy, and the Apollo Theater. Jazz was becoming the unofficial music of the Renaissance, and Duke Ellington and his band wanted to be a part of it.

The dates are not clear, but Duke's Serenaders probably made their first trip to Harlem sometime in 1922. Their drummer, Sonny Greer, scored a gig with a prominent African-American bandleader named Wilbur Sweatman, who had already experienced some success in New York City. Sonny asked if he could bring along his friends and fellow musicians, Duke Ellington and Toby Hardwick. The three of them set off for Harlem to see what they could do. However, after this first gig their work ran out, and so did their money. Instead of getting bookings in the jazz clubs, they began playing "rent parties" out of necessity.

Rent parties were popular social occasions in the African-American community, where tenants hired a musician or band to play for cheap, then asked guests to contribute money toward the "show." Any money left over after paying the musicians went toward the tenants' rent. Because of their popularity in the

Langston Hughes (*front*) and some of his peers who also contributed to the Harlem Renaissance

community, rent parties played a major role in the development of jazz and blues music, but they didn't provide enough income for the Serenaders. The band returned to Washington, where they already had a good reputation, a network of friends, and steady work.

The experience wasn't a complete waste of time, however. Ellington met and made friends with some of the greatest pianists of the day, like Willie "The Lion" Smith and Fats Waller. He also spent time with James P. Johnson, whose playing he had studied in Washington, DC, learning the Harlem Stride from one of its most famous practitioners. The Stride was a highly rhythmic style that required the pianist to keep up a solid rhythm with the left hand while the right hand played the melody and added showy **improvisations**. Duke was already beginning to develop showmanship, and he enjoyed the reaction he would get from the audience when he would briefly lift both hands from the keyboard while playing the Stride.

Having had a taste of what the Big Apple had to offer, Ellington was already planning his return. However, his life was no longer as simple as it had been. He had married his high school sweetheart, Edna Thompson, in 1918. In March 1919, they had a son, Mercer Kennedy Ellington. With a wife and child to support, Ellington decided Washington was the better place to be for the moment.

But then came an opportunity that he couldn't refuse. After Ellington returned from New York City in 1922, Fats Waller came to Washington, DC, to play a show at the Gayety Theatre. Ellington invited Waller to join him at his parents' home for some of his mother's homemade fried chicken. A few weeks later, Waller called Ellington about a job he'd found for the Serenaders in

Duke Ellington and his son, Mercer, posed for a photo in the 1950s.

New York City. In 1923, Duke Ellington transplanted the Serenaders to Harlem, renamed his band the Washingtonians, and began the decade that would define his career.

Duke Ellington spent the first twenty-four years of his life in the culturally strong, tight-knit, African-American community of Washington, DC. In this vibrant atmosphere, encouraged by his parents and supported by friends, he was not only inspired to become a composer and musician, but he learned to take pride in his heritage. He drew from the strength of his people, their vitality, and the spirit of their rich culture.

Professionally, Ellington had learned from a wide variety of teachers, mentors, and other musicians. He had performed in cabarets and restaurants, and at society parties, barn dances, and rent parties. He played for dance classes, fashion shows, and supper shows—in other words, to very different audiences. Ellington had also learned how to lead a band and how to run a musical career like a business. He wasn't yet composing much, if at all, but he had gained tremendous life experience that would help him down the road. He took the confidence he had gained from his mother and the charm he had learned from his father, combined them with his own talents for music and for business, and made a tremendous impact on music for the next five decades.

CHAPTER TWO

THE RIGHT PLACE AT THE RIGHT TIME

The Serenaders were eager to return to Harlem, thanks to Fats Waller, and take advantage of the growing jazz music scene. Sonny Greer, Toby Hardwick, and the rest of the band—without Ellington—left first. They probably rode the Capitol Limited, a famous passenger train run by the Baltimore and Ohio Railroad, which had just started running between New York City and Chicago, Illinois, via Union Station in Washington, DC. Ellington said good-bye to his wife, Edna, and his son, Mercer, a few days later and began his journey.

Like everything he else he did, Ellington rode the train in style. He sat in the parlor car and enjoyed a nice meal in the dining car, which served fresh-made food on linen tablecloths and fine china. When he got to New York City, he **splurged** on a cab to Harlem instead of taking a subway or a bus. Imagine his shock when he met up with Sonny and heard the bad news: the gig Fats Waller helped them get had been canceled.

Opposite: The pocket square, the snazzy suit and tie, and the carefully groomed hair and mustache were all part of Duke Ellington's image.

This time, though, the Serenaders were in luck. Back in Washington, Ellington had met a singer named Ada "Bricktop" Smith—her nickname came from her bright red hair—when he played piano for her at one of her shows. He ran into her shortly after arriving in New York and told her what had happened. Bricktop said she would put in a good word for the Washingtonians with her boss, the owner of a nightclub where she was performing. The name of the nightclub was Barron's Exclusive Club, owned by Mr. Barron Wilkins. Wilkins was quite prominent in the African-American community, and Barron's was one of Harlem's most popular venues. Celebrities such as Babe Ruth, movie star Joan Crawford, and the mayor of New York City spent time there.

The club's patrons were mostly white, and they were required to dress formally, with men wearing jackets and ties, if not tuxedos, and the women wearing evening gowns. The Serenaders may not have been the best band in town, but their image was high-class and fit in with the club's environment. Thanks to Bricktop's introduction, the Washingtonians became the house band at Barron's.

Being the house band meant keeping long hours. Their regular hours started at 11 p.m. and often ended at 10 or 11 the following morning. The money was good, though. They often doubled or tripled their weekly salaries through tips.

Ellington also got a job as the rehearsal pianist at a new club called Connie's Inn, where he learned how to put on a musical **revue**. Connie's Inn was a "black and tan joint," meaning its patrons were both black and white. Its employees and performers were mostly black, and the club offered floor shows with music, dancers, comedians, and other performances.

Up until this point, Ellington had been staying with various friends. Now, with his two jobs, he was financially stable enough to send for his wife. Mercer stayed behind in Washington with Ellington's parents.

While Harlem in 1923 was an exciting place for an African-American performer, it was still a much different place than the sheltered, middle-class, African-American community where Ellington had grown up. In the 1920s, there was no such thing as equal rights for African-American citizens. There were still **lynchings** in the South. Jim Crow laws kept black people and white people separate in most public places. The 1896 Supreme Court ruling that allowed segregation to continue was still in full effect. Race-related riots were common in big cities, and chapters of the Ku Klux Klan—which had begun in the South after the Civil War and the abolition of slavery—began popping up all over the country.

One of the big racial unifiers, though, was music. The Serenaders played mostly background music at Barron's, but they began sneaking some blues and jazz into their repertoire. Both styles were born in the American South, so their growing popularity in the North in the early 1920s was probably due to the Great Migration. Transplanted Southerners were interested in music that reminded them of home. White people were starting to appreciate these new sounds, also.

ANOTHER STEP FORWARD

Once again, luck seems to have played a part in the next big step of Duke Ellington's career. His landlord was producing a show for a place in Times Square called the Hollywood Club. He needed to hire a band, so he asked Duke and the Serenaders if they would take the job. They accepted. It was around this time that they changed their name to the Washingtonians.

At the Hollywood Club, the Washingtonians made more money through better tips. They were also encouraged to play jazz. The Hollywood Club was an after-hours club, located in a basement. It was not the place to play polite background music, like at Barron's. Its customers wanted to hear music that was edgy

An early promotional photo of Duke Ellington and his Orchestra

and exciting; luckily, the Washingtonians underwent major changes during this time that changed their sound for the better. They welcomed new musicians to the band, and those new members helped them to focus on creating an original sound and style.

Around this time, Arthur Whetsol quit the group to go study medicine at Howard University, back in Washington, DC. A trumpeter named James "Bubber" Miley replaced him. Miley brought along his friend, trombone player Charlie "Plug" Irvis. Both Miley and Irvis had unique ways of playing their instruments that resulted in a very distinctive sound. They both used a mute, a device made mostly of rubber that looks rather like a toilet plunger. Placing a mute in the opening of an instrument changes its tone. Moving it in and out creates a "wah wah" effect. Miley also became famous for "growling" while he played, a technique that breaks up the sound of the trumpet and made his performances even more original. Working with Miley and Irvis, Ellington began a habit that he practiced for the rest of his life: he composed songs based on the other musicians in his band and their unique musical talents.

The Washingtonians ended up playing at the Hollywood Club—later renamed the Kentucky Club, or Club Kentucky—for four years. In that time, they added a guitarist, Freddie Guy, when banjo player Elmer Snowden left the band. Plug Irvis moved on in 1926, and another trombonist named Joe "Tricky Sam" Nanton replaced him. One of Ellington's most faithful musicians also came on board in 1926. Seventeen-year-old saxophone player Harry Carney joined as a temporary replacement for Toby Hardwick, and he stayed with Ellington for the next forty-seven years. Saxophonist Johnny Hodges rounded out the group in 1928.

As the Washingtonians went from a six-piece to a ten-piece band, Ellington started to perfect the "Ellington sound," which was about using the power of each individual musician to create a strong whole. The band members all had different talents or preferences, whether it was playing softly or strongly, being more bluesy or more lyrical, or playing faster or slower. Ellington wrote music that brought out the best in each. For example, Johnny Hodges had a smooth, almost liquid playing style. Slow melodies were his forte. Ellington wrote more than one song that would allow Hodges the chance to shine. Ellington would ask Harry Carney to play high notes on his low-pitched baritone sax, which helped to inspire certain moods and emotions. He learned to feature the special sounds that Bubber Miley and Plug Irvis (and, later, Tricky Sam Nanton) created when they played. Two of his most famous compositions, "Black and Tan Fantasy" and "East St. Louis Toodle-Oo," owe a lot to Miley's contributions.

TAKING THE TOWN

More and more, Ellington was becoming the leader of the band, partially because of his abilities as a composer. He cemented this role when a white manager named Irving Mills showed up at the club. Mills told Ellington that the band should be making records. He said he had the connections to get them onto labels that didn't usually put out records made by black musicians. Ellington signed up with Mills, and he brought the rest of the band on board.

Mills became more than a business manager, though. He had a talent for knowing what people wanted to hear, so he worked with Ellington on editing and simplifying some of the band's arrangements. He offered opinions on music and lyrics. His name appears on some of the band's best-selling records, including "Sophisticated Lady." Mills also took credit for launching one of the most important periods in Duke Ellington's career. He got Ellington and the band a contract to play at the Cotton Club.

Duke Ellington and his Orchestra in action. Note the sophisticated outfits worn by all of the musicians.

The Cotton Club had been one of the hottest spots in Harlem for years. It was probably the most famous nightclub in New York, the largest city in America. The club itself was huge and could hold seven hundred **patrons**. The waiters wore tuxedos, and the décor was lush. The nightly shows featured elaborate sets, dramatic lighting, and spectacular costumes. The owner catered to Manhattan's wealthy white crowd, often young, who had money to spare and wanted to "walk on the wild side" while in safe and suitably elegant surroundings.

However, the club was sometimes criticized for the fact that the bandstand was decorated to look like a Southern plantation while the rest of the inside was arranged to look like a jungle. The waiters' tuxedos were red, which some people argued made them look like butlers in a Southern mansion. Writer Langston Hughes, who also rose to prominence during the Harlem Renaissance, publicly voiced disapproval of the way the club was run—especially because the entertainers were African American, and the customers were white only.

Duke Ellington himself never commented on the club's policy of segregation or its racist overtones. He was a realist by necessity. The band needed work, and the money at the Cotton Club was good. He also pointed out in his autobiography that, "as a student of Negro history, I had, in any case, a natural inclination in this direction"—that direction being wild, "jungle" jazz. And the size was definitely an improvement over the Hollywood Club, where the stage was so small that Ellington's piano had to be relocated to the dance floor.

It was during this stint at the Cotton Club that Duke Ellington and his band became the toast of the town. Celebrities and members of high society saw their nightly live shows. They were also broadcast weekly on a radio show, which allowed the entire

Duke Ellington and the Cotton Club Orchestra pose in their tuxedos in 1931.

The Right Place at the Right Time

UNDERWORLD CONNECTIONS

Owney Madden, the owner of the Cotton Club, was a known gangster. He made it very clear to Duke Ellington who was in charge. After he hired Ellington, he wanted the Washingtonians to start right away. Ellington said they had to return to Philadelphia to finish up a contract there. Madden sent a man to talk to the owner of the Philadelphia club; the owner was told, "Be big, or be dead." The owner decided to "be big" about it and released the band from their contract.

Luckily for Ellington, Madden liked him. But that didn't stop a customer from walking up to Ellington one night to demand that the band play "Singin' in the Rain." Ellington was about to refuse when someone told him the man was Legs Diamond, an infamous gangster. As clarinetist Barney Bigard recounted, "The next thing you know, we were playing 'Singin' in the Rain' for a whole hour."

A third gangster, Jerry Sullivan, also took a liking to Ellington. After Ellington received several kidnapping threats, Sullivan drove him to work in his bulletproof car, holding a submachine gun on his lap.

country to listen to their music. Now named the Duke Ellington Orchestra, the band got rave reviews in both local and national newspapers. Tourists began to visit the club to see this band they had heard on the radio and read so much about. Abel Green, a reviewer for *Variety*, wrote, "In Duke Ellington's dance band, Harlem has reclaimed its own after Times Square accepted them … at the Club Kentucky."

During the orchestra's four-year run at the Cotton Club, Ellington composed a remarkable number of songs. He perfected his trademark of using singers' voices as yet another instrument in the songs he wrote. He incorporated African sounds and rhythms into his compositions, so his band continued to sound different from any other band. In fact, nobody else could play Ellington's music quite the way the Duke Ellington Orchestra could. Of course, part of the reason for this was that Ellington tailored his music to the musicians in his band.

There was more to being the house band at the Cotton Club than there was to playing at Club Kentucky. The band was there to do more than provide music for people who wanted to dance. They had to play music for all kinds of singers and other performers, too. This may be how Ellington learned to compose so quickly.

The band introduced some of its most famous tunes during this period, including "Mood Indigo" and "Creole Love Call." The latter was written for Bessie Smith, a singer whose work was also a large part of the Harlem Renaissance. Ellington wrote a song called "Black Beauty" in memory of singer Florence Mills, who had died the month before he started at the club.

In 1929, the Duke Ellington Orchestra appeared simultaneously at the club and in a Broadway production called *Show Girl*, for which George Gershwin had written the music. They also appeared in *Black and Tan*, a nineteen-minute movie that was one of the first to include jazz music. In 1930, they traveled to Hollywood and appeared in a movie called *Check and Double Check* with radio and television performers Amos and Andy. They were onstage at the club, onstage at the theater, on the radio, on the silver screen, and on record players across the world. They experienced real fame as one of the country's most popular big bands, which lasted well into the 1930s.

ON TO THE CONTINENT

By 1931, the era of the Harlem Renaissance was coming to an end. Jazz was no longer the new, hot music that everyone wanted to hear. The Duke Ellington Orchestra was ready for a change. Cab Calloway and his band took over at the Cotton Club, while Ellington's band embarked on a long tour. They added a female singer for the tour, Ivie Anderson, who ended up staying with them for eleven years, and played shows throughout the United States and Europe. In France, they reunited with their old friend Bricktop, who was by then running her own nightclub, and they met President Roosevelt's son, who asked to be introduced to Ellington. In England, they played a private party where the Prince of Wales was not only a guest but sat down at the drums and jammed along with the band, just for fun. In America, it would have been scandalous for a white man, let alone a prince, to play with an African-American band.

The end of the Harlem Renaissance was far from the end of Duke Ellington's career. When the band returned to the United States, they adapted to the current trend of swing music. Swing was a simpler form of jazz, with looser rhythms. Ellington wasn't necessarily interested in writing simpler music, but one of his most popular hit songs was written around this time: "It Don't Mean a Thing (If It Ain't Got That Swing)." "Sophisticated Lady"

Ivie Anderson performs with Duke and the Orchestra, circa 1935.

Duke Ellington

Duke Ellington points to Paul Gonsalves following his famous solo at the 1956 Newport Jazz Festival, which brought the mixed-race crowd to its feet.

was another well-known Ellington tune written during this time. Composer Billy Strayhorn joined the group in 1939 and wrote what would become Ellington's signature song, "Take the 'A' Train." Most of the big bands playing swing featured white musicians led by white bandleaders, like Glenn Miller and Tommy Dorsey. This wasn't really Duke Ellington's scene.

The orchestra toured Europe one more time in the late 1930s, then toured throughout the United States in the 1940s and 1950s. But after World War II, the big band era was over. Some of the orchestra's most prominent members also left the band during the postwar years. Some died, some quit the business, and some joined other bandleaders. It seemed like it might be the end of the Duke Ellington Orchestra altogether.

Then, in 1956, the band was invited to perform at the Newport Jazz Festival. They played some new music, a few old favorites, and ended the show with a performance that brought the crowd to its feet. The piece was called "Diminuendo and Crescendo in Blue," and it was not new. They had played it many times before. However, because some of the musicians were different, the improvisations and solos were different, so the song had a whole new sound. At one point, Ellington told saxophonist Paul Gonsalves to "blow as long as he wanted" during his solo. Gonsalves whipped the crowd into a frenzy by playing an intense solo for twenty-seven choruses. The audience clapped and screamed, and the show went on long after its expected conclusion. The album produced after the show, *Ellington at Newport*, was his all-time biggest seller. Duke Ellington and his orchestra stormed back into the American consciousness, and they never left it again.

Once, when Ellington was asked about his decade in New York City and his contributions to the era known as the Harlem Renaissance, he answered, "I was the right guy, in the right place, at the right time, doing the right thing." On the one hand, that statement sounds like he is making light of his talent, his hard work, and all of his accomplishments. On the other hand, it's true—Duke Ellington struck a chord in American culture at just the right time.

Duke Ellington's birthplace, his family, his creativity, and his confidence made him the right guy to enter the Harlem community in the 1920s and tap into what was happening there. As for the right time, the Harlem Renaissance **encompassed** some of the most significant intellectual and artistic trends of twentieth-century American history. The people involved embraced and promoted black heritage and culture in American life. Duke Ellington's ability to incorporate blues, jazz, and African sounds into his music made him an important part of that movement. As for doing the right thing, he wrote more than three thousand songs during his lifetime. He composed music for Broadway, the ballet, the church, Hollywood, and other venues. His songs have been used in movies for decades. People all over the world know his music, without necessarily knowing that it's his.

CHAPTER THREE

THE OTHER SIDE OF THE COIN

Duke Ellington was an accomplished, beloved, famous musician known all over the world. There's no denying that he experienced a tremendous amount of success and made an incredible impact on American music. However, not everything was easy for him as an African-American man living in America in the early and mid-twentieth century, and his personal life was less than perfect.

RACISM AND SEGREGATION

Duke Ellington rose to fame years before the civil rights movement. Jim Crow laws, pro-segregation policies, and the white community's general ignorance of the struggles of the African-American community all affected him the same as they affected any other man of color.

For example, when Ellington and his orchestra took on the job of house band at the Cotton Club, it had strict rules about who was allowed in and who wasn't. White people were the only

Opposite: This Pullman train car, shown here during the day, could be converted to a sleeper car.

The Pullman car revolutionized train travel.

customers allowed. The best African-American talent could be performing on stage, but their friends were not allowed through the front doors. Ellington's own mother was not allowed to attend his shows and sit in the audience.

In 1931, when Ellington and Irving Mills decided to hire a female singer to accompany the band, Ivie Anderson was not their first choice. They had wanted to hire a different woman, but that woman was so **light-skinned** that she appeared white, especially in contrast with some of the band members. It would have been unheard of for a white woman to be onstage with a black band, so although the woman was not actually white, they had to hire Anderson, whose skin was darker.

Two years later, the Duke Ellington Orchestra traveled to England for the first time. While there, they ran into a problem they must not have anticipated: not all of them were welcome in London's hotels. As the story goes, a newspaper reporter actually called several hotels to see whether they would accept black guests. The manager of one place replied, "We can put one up for the night if he's well behaved." Another inquired how dark the guest's skin was. Due to this unexpected racism, the light-skinned Ellington was allowed to stay in a city hotel room, while the rest of the band had to stay elsewhere.

This is one of the reasons Ellington refused to take the band on a tour through the South for many years. He knew that they would be forced to stay in separate hotels, use separate bathrooms and water fountains, eat in different areas of restaurants (if they were allowed to eat in white restaurants at all), and generally be treated with a lack of respect. That was not the world he was used to, and he did not want to experience it.

When Ellington eventually agreed to tour Southern cities, he and the band came up with a way to get around many of those problems. Instead of staying in hotels, they set up residence on train cars and in Pullman cars, specifically, which were luxurious and included beds. They had their own water, food, electricity, and restrooms. Ellington liked to tell people, "That's the way the President travels." No matter what kind of spin he put on it, however, the truth was that traveling like this was the only way these talented musicians could avoid being treated as inferiors.

Even in larger cities in the North during later years, Ellington and his band experienced racism. Many African-American soldiers fought and died for their country in World War II. Yet during the war years, when the Duke Ellington Orchestra played at the Fox Theatre in St. Louis, they had trouble finding cab drivers who would take them to the theater from the train station. When they needed food between shows, they couldn't find restaurants that would serve them. They ended up having to send a white person to a local lunch counter to buy them sandwiches.

Ellington faced criticism from other African-American performers and activists for his refusal to take a stand. Singer Lena Horne, for example, once walked out on a show at an army base in Arkansas when she realized that African-American soldiers were not allowed to attend. When the governor of Arkansas defied a court order and prevented African-American students from attending white schools, the great jazz trumpeter Louis Armstrong publicly spoke out against him. In the 1960s, when comedian and civil rights activist Dick Gregory urged Ellington to appear at the March on Washington—where Martin Luther King Jr. gave his famous "I Have a Dream" speech—Ellington turned him down.

Publicly, he said he preferred to let his music do the talking for him. In addition to a jazz symphony he composed in 1943 about racism called *Black, Brown, and Beige*, Ellington wrote the music for *My People*, a 1963 show about the African-American struggle for freedom. Privately, he had another opinion of people who were fighting, and risking their lives, for civil rights in the South: "Those cats are crazy." This opinion certainly was not popular with those who wanted freedom from racism and segregation. But Ellington knew that his continued popularity and ability to earn money depended on him not making waves.

DUKE AND HIS MOTHER

Ellington's mother, Daisy, was one of the strongest influences in his life. Duke himself admitted that she had always spoiled him. True to the times, she did not work but stayed home to devote herself to her son and, later, her daughter. She constantly told her son that he was special and blessed, never punished him, and denied him very little.

To my dear little Henry from Aunt Daisy

A rare photograph of Daisy Ellington, Duke Ellington's beloved mother

If Ellington got sick, his mother would send for two doctors, not just one. When he was five, she lied about his age to enroll him in school, then followed him there almost every day to make sure he was safe. Today, she would be called a "helicopter parent," always hovering over her child. There may have been a reason for her extreme levels of concern and care: she had lost another child before Duke was born. Whatever her reasons, Daisy helped supply the young Duke with his legendary confidence, but her devotion to him also caused problems in his other relationships.

Daisy and Duke Ellington's relationship stayed strong throughout the latter's adulthood. She moved in with him and his wife when they were having problems. Her goal was to lessen the stress of an unhappy marriage on her son. She felt he needed peace and quiet, and she didn't want him to face difficult conflicts. When that marriage abruptly ended, Daisy left her husband in Washington, DC, and rushed to her son's side in New York City. She helped him find a new place to live and moved in with him. He bought her a Pierce Arrow sedan and hired a chauffeur to drive her around. The rest of the family—his father, sister, and son—also moved to New York shortly thereafter, and they all shared an apartment for many years.

Daisy Ellington was diagnosed with cancer in the fall of 1934, and she passed away the following spring. Her son was devastated. He ordered three thousand flowers for her funeral and bought a casket that cost $3,500. This was at a time when many families lived on less than $2,000 a year.

Her death sent Duke into a deep depression. Mercer Ellington later described his father's feelings about his loss: "His world had been built around his mother, and the days after her death were the saddest and most morbid of his life ... He just sat around the house and wept for days." Duke recorded very little music and wrote almost nothing in the worst days of his grief, which was unusual for him. He said, "I have no ambition left. The bottom's out of everything."

He did eventually return to work, writing a piece dedicated to his mother called **Reminiscing** in Tempo. He never stopped missing her, though. He never wore the color brown again because he'd been wearing brown clothing the day she died. After her death, he would also say that he hated the color green because it reminded him of cemeteries. At a White House reception in 1969, more than thirty years later, he commented that "there is no place I would rather be tonight, except in my mother's arms."

DUKE AND HIS WIFE

Ellington was only married once. Like his mother, Edna Thompson was light-skinned, beautiful, and musical—she played the piano and wanted to teach music. Also like Daisy, Thompson and her family came from a higher level of black society. She once said that, according to her parents, Ellington and his family were never good enough for her.

Thompson also said that they were too young to get married, and they probably wouldn't have, except that she discovered she was pregnant. Mercer Kennedy Ellington was born about eight months after their wedding. He was their only living child.

Thompson and Ellington fought constantly and abruptly separated in 1928 after nine years of marriage. Thompson often accused Ellington of being **unfaithful** to her, and finally she had enough. In a fit of anger, she slashed the left side of her husband's face with a razor. That night, Ellington walked out of the apartment and never went back.

However, they never divorced. This may have been due to Ellington's religious upbringing, or it may have been a convenient excuse not to marry any subsequent girlfriends. He paid for

Ellington celebrating his sixty-fifth birthday with Evie Ellis.

Thompson's apartment and probably gave her money for their son's upbringing, but he never talked about her publicly. He didn't even mention her in his autobiography.

Thirty years later, in 1959, a writer with *Ebony* magazine tracked Thompson down for an interview. She answered questions about their marriage and discussed Ellington's **infidelity**, among other things. When it was published, Ellington was furious, but the damage was already done. His wife—never officially his ex-wife—was no longer a secret.

Ellington must have eventually forgiven Thompson. When she died in 1966, he released a polite statement to the media: "[Edna] loved life. She was a woman of virtue and beauty. She would never lie. God bless her."

RELATIONSHIPS WITH OTHER WOMEN

After he separated from Thompson, Ellington began a new relationship with a Cotton Club dancer named Mildred Dixon. She lived with him, his parents, his sister, and his son for a time. Daisy Ellington treated her like a daughter-in-law. But just like he had done with Thompson, Duke never talked about Dixon in public.

Dixon and Ellington were together for several years. She was with him throughout his depression after his mother died. But he left her soon after for a woman named Evie Ellis, who also worked at the Cotton Club. Ellis and Ellington stayed together for the rest of his life, and she sometimes referred to herself as Mrs. Ellington, although he never married her. Even after Edna Thompson's death, he refused to get married again. He also cheated on Ellis, although not as much as he had cheated on Thompson.

When Ellis died, not long after Ellington did, she was buried at the same gravesite. However, her name doesn't appear on

Mercer Ellington played trumpet in his father's orchestra for a time.

his tombstone. This only completed the pattern Duke Ellington established during his life; he never gave any women he was close to, except his mother and his sister, any respect.

DUKE AND HIS SON

Mercer Ellington was Duke's only child, but he was not spoiled. In fact, he didn't see a lot of his father in his early years.

Duke first moved to New York from Washington, DC, in 1923, when Mercer was only four years old. When his mother moved to Harlem to be with his father, she left Mercer behind to live with his paternal grandparents. He didn't move in with his parents until he was eight years old, although he used to see them on his summer vacations. Mercer was able to take some trips with the band as he got older, but he always wondered why he didn't get more time and attention from his father, even when they finally lived together.

When his parents broke up, he was too young to know the details, but nobody even bothered to tell Mercer that his father had moved out. He remembered coming home from school not long after the incident with the razor—which he did not know about at the time—to discover that his father had moved his new girlfriend, Mildred Dixon, into the apartment that Mercer now shared with his grandparents, his aunt Ruth, and Duke. He shrugged it off, saying, "Nobody in my family liked to be the bearer of good news," but he must have known by that point that his father didn't consider his feelings when making decisions. When Duke left Dixon to live with Ellis, Mercer was left to live with his aunt Ruth.

Much later, when Mercer was old enough to join the Duke Ellington Orchestra as a trumpet player, Duke never acknowledged him onstage as his son. He did usually end shows with a song that Mercer had written, "Things Ain't What They Used to Be," but as far as their professional relationship went, Mercer was just another member of the band. Trumpeter Rex Stewart once recalled being at a recording section in 1966 where Duke asked, "Where's the other trumpet player?" He meant Mercer. That may be why Mercer called him Duke, not Dad.

Even in his autobiography, Ellington's compliments for his son came in the form of compliments for himself. He wrote in one chapter, "My son, Mercer Ellington, is dedicated to maintaining the luster of his father's image." He also said, "Mercer is always up straight and standing tall in defense of Duke Ellington."

Instead of enjoying his son, Ellington seems to have felt competitive with him. Some music historians claim that Ellington was upset that his son was a boy instead of a girl. When Mercer decided that he wanted to be a musician, his father paid for him to go to Juilliard, then criticized his son for pursuing formal music education. When Mercer started his own band, he claimed that his father stole good musicians away from him and told his record label to release inferior versions of Mercer's songs.

Mercer did take on the role of manager of the Duke Ellington Orchestra in the 1960s, and after his father died, he became the leader of the band. Like everybody else, he seems to have respected his father's talents as a musician, but not as a parent.

THE END OF AN ERA

By the end of the 1960s, Ellington was beginning to feel depressed about his life and his career. His collaborator and friend Billy Strayhorn died from cancer. Many of his other bandmates were ill or required surgery. Johnny Hodges, who had been with the Duke Ellington Orchestra for more than forty years, had to leave the band after suffering heart problems. He died of a heart attack

A SUPERSTITIOUS MAN

Although Duke Ellington appeared to be sophisticated and educated, he was also extremely superstitious and quirky. He hated to fly, so whenever he had to, he could be seen clutching the gold cross his sister had given him. He would not allow peanuts, newspapers, or whistling backstage—not allowing whistling backstage is a well-known theatrical superstition, but who knows what he had against peanuts and newspapers? Ellington refused to wear a watch because he didn't want to "rush through life." During a rainstorm, he would insist that all windows be closed so no lightning could enter the room. He would never wear a jacket again after a button had dropped off. He said he hated the color green because it reminded him of cemeteries, and he would never again wear brown after his mother passed away, because that was the color of his outfit on the day she died. According to his son, Ellington wouldn't buy socks or shoes for anyone because he said it would cause them to "walk away from him." He was terrified of traveling on the ocean because of the *Titanic* disaster, so when he had to travel to England aboard the RMS *Olympic*, nobody dared tell him that the *Olympic* was the *Titanic*'s sister ship.

A pensive Duke Ellington, circa 1950

the following year. Ellington, who had been grief-stricken when Strayhorn died, came right out and said, "Johnny is not replaceable. Because of this great loss, our band will never sound the same."

Ellington himself was starting to slow down. His once limitless energy was gone. Even his public persona, which had always been warm, charming, and friendly, became more reserved.

He took the time to write his autobiography, in which he glossed over the difficulties of his life and never mentioned his important romantic relationships. And in true Duke Ellington style, he threw a fit when the first printings of the book featured a brown cover. Brown was the color he had hated since his mother died. He insisted that it be reprinted in blue.

Yet Ellington never stopped working. He composed a score for a ballet for the American Ballet Theatre, which premiered at Lincoln Center with choreography by Alvin Ailey. He wrote a piece called *Afro-Eurasian Eclipse*, which he played at the 1970 Monterey Jazz Festival, and he worked on three Sacred Concerts. The first two were played at St. John the Divine in New York City. The third had its premiere at Westminster Abbey in London in 1973. He was so tired at this performance, though, that he actually had to leave the stage when there was no piano part.

What many people didn't know, because Ellington was such a private person, was that he had been diagnosed with lung cancer about ten years earlier. Somehow, he had kept going—although he didn't quit smoking! By the middle of 1974, Duke Ellington's body was starting to give out. He checked into Columbia Presbyterian Hospital, and brought a piano with him. When he could no longer play the piano, he dictated notes into a tape recorder. His son was also at his side, helping him. He was literally composing until the day he died.

Two of Ellington's bandmates, Tyree Glenn and Paul Gonsalves, died just days before he did. Nobody had the heart to tell Ellington. A few months after Ellington's own death, Harry Carney, the sax player who had been with him longer than anyone else, also died. The glory days of the Duke Ellington Orchestra were well and truly over.

Flowers covered the casket and the altar at Duke Ellington's funeral service, held at St. John the Divine Episcopal Cathedral in New York City, on May 27, 1974.

Duke Ellington died on May 24, 1974. He was barely seventy-five years old. The response to his death was tremendous. Sixty-five thousand people came to pay their respects. The funeral home had to stay open twenty-four hours a day. Thousands of **condolence** calls and telegrams arrived. President Richard Nixon said, "The wit, taste, intelligence, and elegance that Duke Ellington brought to his music have made him, in the eyes of millions of people both here and abroad, America's foremost composer." It was his longtime friend, singer Ella Fitzgerald, who may have summed it up best: "It's a very sad day. A genius has passed."

Ten thousand people packed the Cathedral of St. John the Divine for Ellington's funeral. Attendees included jazz musicians Benny Goodman and Count Basie, and singers Lena Horne, Tony Bennett, and Joe Williams. Frank Sinatra sent a large floral arrangement. Thousands more people stood outside, listening to a broadcast of the service on speakers. An old friend of Ellington's gave the **eulogy**. Ella Fitzgerald sang, and Earl Hines played the piano. The service ended with a recording from the *Second Sacred Concert*, which Ellington had composed just a few years earlier. When it was all over, Ellington was buried next to his parents in Woodlawn Cemetery in the Bronx, in his adopted city of New York.

Music was always more important to Duke Ellington than anything else, including his own family. His musical genius did lead to fame and fortune, but that fame came at a price. He put almost all of himself into his music, and he didn't have much left for other people or relationships. He was wealthy and talented, but he was unable to maintain healthy relationships with anyone around him. His wife, Edna Thompson, once described him as "a lonely man. He masks his emotions. Never wants you to know how he actually feels."

Maybe the man said it best himself in his autobiography: "Music is my mistress, and she plays second fiddle to no one ... Lovers have come and gone, but only my mistress stays."

PART II

The Works of Duke Ellington

"There are simply two kinds of music, good music and the other kind ... The only yardstick by which the result should be judged is simply that of how it sounds. If it sounds good, it's successful; if it doesn't, it has failed."

—Duke Ellington in
Where Is Music Going? (1962)

Opposite: Duke Ellington and President Richard M. Nixon, after Nixon presented Ellington with the Presidential Medal of Freedom in 1969

CHAPTER FOUR

A LIFETIME OF MUSIC

Duke Ellington's name is **synonymous** with jazz music, but he never liked to be labeled as a jazz musician—or anything else. This may have been an effect of his upbringing in segregated Washington, DC, where not only whites and African Americans were separated, but where there were different classes and statuses within the African-American community itself. Whatever the cause, Ellington rejected labels on both himself and his music for his entire life.

In his career of more than fifty years, Ellington composed thousands of songs. He **synthesized** many elements of American popular music—from minstrel songs and ragtime, to Tin Pan Alley, the blues, and American versions of European musical traditions. He wrote three-minute songs for recordings and a forty-five minute piece for a jazz symphony, and everything from romantic ballads to foot-stomping melodies that inspired people to dance the night away. Within the framework of ragtime, jazz, and the blues, he created a unique sound and an incredible portfolio of music.

Opposite: Shown here composing at the piano, Ellington was known to compose just about anywhere, any time.

THE ELLINGTON SOUND

Duke Ellington created and maintained one of the most distinctive ensembles in the world through his unique style of composing—what has been called the "Ellington Effect."

The seeds of the Ellington Effect were planted back in the early 1920s. When Ellington first arrived in Harlem, his goal was to be a songwriter. By the time the Duke Ellington Orchestra became the house band at the Cotton Club, he'd become a composer.

From those early days on, Ellington worked with compatible musicians who liked his improvisational style of writing and playing music. Many of his early hits list Bubber Miley as a cowriter. Miley and Ellington both created "tone pictures" when they wrote songs. For example, Miley created the idea behind the melody of "East St. Louis Toodle-Oo." He was trying to express in music what he imagined a tired old man limping home after a long day at work would feel.

Ellington found sources of inspiration everywhere. Sometimes his songs depict places ("Echoes of Harlem" and "Isfahan") or people ("Jack the Bear," named after a Harlem bass player that Ellington knew, and "Portrait of the Lion," a tribute to stride piano player Willie "The Lion" Smith). Sometimes they were about nature ("Dusk" and "Sunset and the Mockingbird") or emotions ("Melancholia" and "Mood Indigo"). Sometimes, he simply wrote songs about things he liked, such as trains ("Daybreak Express" and "Happy-Go-Lucky Local").

One of his lesser-known works, "Immigration Blues," paints the picture of both sides of the immigration experience. The song starts off in a very Southern, folk-culture style, with a religious and spiritual feel. The second half of the song has a more bluesy feel to represent the sadness and longing of the relocated Southerner.

Ellington's songwriting also may have been influenced by his early study of art. He had a visual imagination, and he often

This 1943 portrait of the Duke Ellington Orchestra includes singer Ivie Anderson.

ELLINGTON'S EXCEPTIONAL MUSICIANS

In the 1920s and 1930s, the members of most bands or orchestras never stayed with one group for long. Musicians moved from band to band. Yet, when a musician played with Duke Ellington, he usually stayed, sometimes for many years. Many of the musicians who played with Duke Ellington over the years were incredibly loyal. Here is a list of those musicians who stayed with Duke for more than ten years:

Harry Carney, baritone sax, 1927–1974
Russell Procope, clarinet, 1945–1974
Billy Strayhorn, collaborator, 1938–1967 (his death)
Sonny Greer, drums, 1923–1951
Paul Gonsalves, tenor sax, 1950–1974
Freddie Guy, banjo, 1925–1949
Johnny Hodges, alto sax, 1928–1951
Ray Nance, trumpet, 1940–1963
Cootie Williams, trumpet, 1929–1940; 1962–1974
Tricky Sam Nanton, trombone, 1926–1946
Lawrence Brown, trombone, 1932–1951
Otto Hardwick, alto sax, 1923–1928, 1932–1946
Juan Tizol, trombone, 1929–1944
Barney Bigard, clarinet, 1927–1942
Ivie Anderson, vocalist, 1931–1942
Rex Stewart, cornet, 1934–1945
Ben Webster, saxophone, 1935–1943
Wellman Braud, bass, 1927–1935

Two other musicians who played significant roles in Ellington's orchestra were Jimmy Blanton (bass) and Arthur Whetsol (trumpet). Both probably would have spent long stints with Ellington, but they died young.

described composing in terms of color. He was once heard telling a musician to soften his sound by making it "pastel."

Another reason Duke Ellington's songs were so different was his method of composition. He wrote songs everywhere, from hotel rooms to train cars to buses. He would bring the pieces to the band in the recording studio, to afternoon rehearsals, or even to be played onstage that night. The band was his testing ground and his "laboratory," where he could experiment with new ideas and make changes immediately until the performed song matched what he heard in his head. Musicians who couldn't function within this type of improvisational environment would leave the band.

To complicate matters further, Ellington didn't always write things down. When he did, he usually didn't indicate which instrument should be played. Instead, he'd note which musician would play each part. That's because he didn't write for an instrument, but for his individual band members and their particular musical talents. He would often switch parts as the music was rehearsed until it sounded right to him. Ellington was once compared to classical composer Franz Joseph Haydn, who also had an orchestra at his disposal. He was the only modern bandleader who composed, arranged, and directed an orchestra that he personally shaped almost every step of the way. He had the good luck to hear his music played almost as soon as it was written.

Billy Strayhorn may have been the first band member to express Ellington's style in words. He described it this way: "Ellington plays the piano, but his real instrument is the band. Each member of his band is to him a distinctive tone color and set of emotions, which he mixes with others equally distinctive to produce a third thing, which I like to call the Ellington Effect."

The Ellington Effect was created through both necessity and desire. It was necessary due to Ellington's lack of formal musical training. It was desirable because he wanted to create a different sound from everyone else's dance music. When he had to hire new musicians, he chose them based on their distinctive sounds and individual personalities.

Another facet of the Ellington Effect was that Ellington would come up with unusual combinations of instruments to create sounds people hadn't heard before. He'd pair saxophones with tubas. He'd use an entire section of one instrument to play a solo. Sometimes his musicians were surprised at the parts they were asked to play in a piece, expecting that another instrument would be "right" for that line.

The Ellington Effect played a huge role in the band's success. Most of the bands they were competing with used the "call and response" style. Brass instruments and reed instruments would face off against each other. One side would play part of the song—the call—then the other would play it back—the response. Ellington blended the instruments instead. He said this gave the music more color and more emotional impact.

Don George was one of the lyricists who worked with Ellington. He said, "Duke had a strange way of composing. Most tune writers wrote the melody first, then worked out the chord structure behind it, but Duke wrote the chords and that was that." George was pleasantly surprised at how Ellington made it all work, though: "At first I felt as though I was feeling my way through a labyrinth and had forgotten to unwind the string behind me that would return me to the entrance; but gradually, through some form of musical osmosis, the words fell in the right places and lo! … We had a song."

The Ellington Effect also had a negative side. Because it was created so specifically, Ellington's music never sounds quite right when played by other groups, no matter how good the musicians are. As one industry saying goes, "Separating the Ellington sound from the Ellington band was impossible."

Also, because of the way he put together songs and brought in different ideas and elements, there was sometimes controversy over songwriting credits. The song "Sophisticated Lady" created one

Duke Ellington and Billy Strayhorn, 1948. They had wildly different personalities but a prolific writing partnership.

such example. Ellington claimed he wrote it, but Otto Hardwick and trombonist Lawrence Brown actually composed much of the music together. When the song was first recorded, the two received credit along with Ellington. By the time the song was copyrighted, their names were no longer on the piece, and they didn't receive royalties.

Juan Tizol, who played trombone in Ellington's band for fifteen years, came up with the main themes for two of the band's well-known songs, "Caravan" and "Perdido." Johnny Hodges was the source for "Never No Lament," which later became "Don't Get Around Much Anymore." Cootie Williams's "Concerto for Cootie" developed into "Do Nothin' Till You Hear from Me." Some of the musicians resented Ellington for portraying himself as the composer on all of these songs. Billy Strayhorn, who collaborated with Ellington for twenty-eight years, grew resentful when he realized he would never get full credit for his contributions. While Ellington often mentioned Strayhorn's involvement in songs when they were played live, he often left him off the credits when songs were recorded.

Ellington, however, never seemed to think there was anything wrong with this arrangement; he said that he was happy to share credit with other musicians when the piece didn't require him to do too much extra work to "fit the band." Another trombonist, Lawrence Brown, called it "musical kleptomania." Brown once accused Ellington of being not a composer but a compiler. Tizol, however, shrugged it off: "Oh, he'd steal like mad, no questions about it. He'd steal from his own self."

A NEW DIRECTION

In the mid-1920s, Ellington and his orchestra produced three recordings that showed they were taking jazz music in a new direction. These songs prominently displayed the band's unique sound.

The first of these songs was "Black and Tan Fantasy." It featured Bubber Miley's two distinctive styles: his growling and his wah-wah sound. Although on the surface the song was about the atmosphere of black and tan clubs like Connie's Inn, it was more blues than jazz. It also reflected Miley's Southern roots and a deep sense of spirituality. Although he'd been born and raised in New York City, Miley's family came from the Deep South. He incorporated themes from spiritual songs that his mother used to sing to him. The sounds and themes that Bubber Miley contributed to the song made it stand out from the competition. People who heard it, even those without musical training, could tell they were hearing something different—and they liked it.

The second song, "Creole Love Call," puzzled listeners at first. They thought they were hearing another growling horn in the mix, but it turned out to be the voice of singer Adelaide Hall. Most other jazz composers wouldn't use vocals as an instrument for decades. Hall wasn't singing words, but vocalizing a countermelody that she had actually created herself. She'd been traveling with the band on the theater circuit when she first heard them play the tune, and she started humming an improvised countermelody. Apparently Ellington told her that he liked what she'd done and asked her to do it again. He brought her onstage to perform the song with the band that night, then brought her into the studio the next day so she could record her contribution.

The third song, "East St. Louis Toodle-Oo," was a huge hit. It served as Ellington's theme song for more than ten years. It's been called "one of the most completely realized jazz recordings of the mid-twenties." Yet, it had a very different sound. It starts off in a minor key, with the tuba and saxophone paired up to create an eerie, mysterious effect. The next section, written in a major key, has almost polka-like rhythms. Bubber Miley, who received co-composer credit, created the main theme of the tune and also gave himself a long, bluesy plunger solo.

When asked what inspired him to write, Ellington once replied, "My men and my race are the inspiration of my work. I try to catch the character and mood and feeling of my people." He echoed his response when asked about the contrasts between the minor and major keys in "East St. Louis Toodle-Oo." He claimed it was due to his race: "You know how the Negroes are. They pass quickly from the extremes of joy to gloom and back again. There must be the same quality in pure Negro music."

BEST-KNOWN WORKS

Duke Ellington left behind more than three thousand songs when he died. With so many works to choose from, it's almost impossible to narrow down the list to his most significant works. However, there are certain pieces that almost everyone has heard, whether in a concert, a class, a movie, or even a commercial.

"It Don't Mean a Thing (If It Ain't Got That Swing)"

In the 1930s, swing music suddenly became popular, and bandleader Benny Goodman earned the nickname "The King of Swing." Ellington wasn't a fan of the style. He said it was just another type of jazz and that "swing" was the Harlem term for "rhythm." He named this song after a saying he credited to James "Bubber" Miley: "If it ain't worth singing, it ain't worth swinging. If it ain't worth swinging, it ain't worth playing." The song helped define Miley's growling brass sound that became one of the band's trademarks. It also features chanting brass figures and an alto saxophone solo by Johnny Hodges that was ahead of its time. It was the first recording that Ivie Anderson made with the band. She made the song a standout in live performances.

"Mood Indigo"

"Mood Indigo" made Ellington internationally famous. Fitting its name, "Mood Indigo" has a blues-like character and a slow tempo.

This song is notable to musicians because Ellington's scoring was so unconventional. The clarinet, trumpet, and trombone carry the melody, but they switch their usual roles. The clarinet plays the low voice, the trumpet plays the middle, and the muted trombone takes on the high voice. The song was meant to **evoke** the feeling of someone waiting for his sweetheart to come by, only the sweetheart never shows up. It was the Duke Ellington Orchestra's first big hit. Ellington once claimed he wrote it in only fifteen minutes.

"In a Sentimental Mood"

This yearning, haunting melody was the fourth of Ellington's songs to become a pop standard. He wrote it in 1933, shortly after returning from the orchestra's first European tour. His mother had recently been diagnosed with cancer, which probably contributed to the song's melancholy feeling. Toby Hardwick, however, wrote the first eight bars. "In a Sentimental Mood" rose to number fourteen on the pop charts. It was used as the theme song for nine different radio shows. Praise from music critics included comments like "simply the most beautiful song ever written" and "the perfect soundtrack for falling in love."

"Sophisticated Lady"

Duke Ellington and his orchestra's recording of this song entered the pop charts on May 27, 1933, and stayed there for sixteen weeks, rising to number three. As with many Ellington songs, "Sophisticated Lady" started out as an instrumental piece. The lyrics were written later. There is a dispute as to who actually wrote the melody for "Sophisticated Lady." Lawrence Brown says he wrote the first eight bars and also credits Toby Hardwick. The initial set of composer credits listed Ellington, Hardwick, Brown, and Mills, but when the song was published, the credits only named Ellington and Mills. Hardwick and Brown received no credit and no royalties.

Duke Ellington and his Orchestra, in the early days, wearing formal white ties.

"Don't Get Around Much Anymore"

This song was first released in 1940 as "Never No Lament." By 1943, lyrics had been added and the title was changed. The song tells the story of a jilted lover who prefers to stay home rather than be haunted by memories of happier times spent at dances and nightspots. Once the tune was released as "Don't Get Around Much Anymore," it hit the charts and stayed there for sixteen weeks.

"Solitude"

In his autobiography, Duke Ellington told the story of how the song "Solitude" was created: "We had arrived in a Chicago recording studio … with three numbers ready and a fourth needed. The band ahead of us went into overtime … so, standing up, leaning against the studio's glass enclosure, I wrote the score of 'Solitude' in twenty minutes." Trumpeter Cootie Williams confirmed that the song was totally an Ellington composition with no contributions from other band members—except for one: trumpeter Arthur Whetsol is credited with giving the tune its title. "Solitude" was a successful song, both in record and sheet music sales. Ella Fitzgerald sang "Solitude" at Duke Ellington's funeral.

"Take the 'A' Train"

The song that became the signature tune of the Duke Ellington Orchestra, "Take the 'A' Train" marked the beginning of a decades-long partnership between Ellington and a shy young songwriter named Billy Strayhorn. Strayhorn claimed the title comes from stories about the New York City subway system. He said he would hear stories from Harlem-bound housewives who took the 'D' train by accident and ended up in the Bronx, because only the 'A' train went to Sugar Hill in Harlem. Another story says the title came from directions Ellington gave Strayhorn on how to get to Ellington's Harlem apartment. Strayhorn also said that the song was "born without any effort—it was like writing a song to a friend." When "Take the 'A' Train" was recorded, trumpeter Ray Nance's trumpet solo would become the best known of his career. That solo became so essential to the song that he played it the exact same way every time—and the band played this song almost every night. Nance also led several other musicians in playing a slow, serious version of this song at Billy Strayhorn's funeral.

Dancer Virgil Gadson (*bottom left*), singer Patti LaBelle (*center left*), actor Dulé
Hill (*right*) and the ensemble of *After Midnight* brought down the house at the
Broadway show's final curtain call in 2014.

Duke Ellington originally wrote the melody for this song, which at first was an instrumental piece. Billy Strayhorn added in harmony and lyrics and named it "Satin Doll," which was his pet name for his mother. Later, Johnny Mercer wrote new lyrics, resulting in the song we know today. "Satin Doll" is unique among Ellington compositions because it was not written with a particular soloist in mind. Ellington himself played the introductory piano solo.

A LASTING IMPACT

Duke Ellington's impact on jazz and American music was immediate and long lasting. He led his various bands from 1926 to 1974 and consistently ranked among the top five performing artists during all those years. He was prolific, innovative, collaborative, and always an original. Duke Ellington and his orchestra have impacted American culture so deeply that even if you aren't familiar with the Duke, you have probably heard his music.

CHAPTER FIVE

A LIFETIME OF PROFESSIONAL SUCCESS

Imagine celebrating your seventieth birthday at the White House. Now imagine that having your birthday celebration there was the president's idea. This is exactly what happened to Duke Ellington. The guest list included composers Harold Arlen and Richard Rodgers, bandleader Benny Goodman, singer Billy Eckstine, fellow pianist and bandleader Count Basie, singer and bandleader Cab Calloway, and trumpeter Dizzy Gillespie. Politicians from the vice president to members of the cabinet joined Ellington's family and friends. Dinner was a white-tie affair, followed by President Nixon presenting Ellington with the Presidential Medal of Freedom, the highest honor the United States government can bestow on a civilian. The citation the president read stated, "In the royalty of American music, no man swings more or stands higher than the Duke."

Of course, the evening included musical entertainment, kicked off by President Nixon sitting at the piano and playing "Happy Birthday." Ellington himself played a few pieces on the piano.

Opposite: President Richard M. Nixon played and sang "Happy Birthday" to Duke Ellington at the composer's seventieth birthday celebration, held at the White House.

The United States Marine Band played. Jazz pianists Earl Hines, Dave Brubeck, and Billy Taylor all performed, as did singers Joe Williams and Mary Mayo. This was such an important gathering that the musical portion of the evening was broadcast over the government's radio channel, Voice of America.

The party ended in the wee hours of the morning. Ellington went back to his hotel room, changed out of his tuxedo, put on traveling clothes, and left for the airport. He was due in Oklahoma City that night for a concert, and he was, after all, a working musician.

CRITICAL ACCLAIM

Indeed, Duke Ellington was a star on both the American and European music scenes for decades. As opposed to some composers who work in **obscurity** for years or only score a handful of hits— or even just one—Ellington racked up an astonishing number of successes in a career that spanned more than fifty years.

The critics were almost always kind, at least in the early days. For example, in the early 1920s, the *Fall River Herald News* in Fall River, Massachusetts, published an article stating, "This prince of melody and his band scored a tremendous hit ... Duke Ellington and his galaxy of Broadway stars are now engaged in a whirlwind tour of the New England states ... Ellington, pianist and director of this entertaining orchestra, is one of the nation's foremost figures in the musical world. The inimitable presentation of the Southland's crooning melodies, masterfully blended with modern-day jazz, will completely captivate everyone."

A 1927 piece in the *New York Tribune* also raved about the band, saying they were "taking the territory by storm." The story went on: "There is nothing unusual about this orchestra, yet, when you start dancing you don't want to stop." It concluded that the band "simply sweep you off your feet." The same year, the *Portland Press Herald* in Maine said, "Bring Your Asbestos Ear

Muffs to Hear the Hottest Blue Blowing Dance Band above the Earth!" With reviews like this, it's no wonder that positive word of mouth about Duke and his band spread throughout the country.

A rare exception occurred during the band's first trip to Great Britain. During the first half of one concert, the audience seemed to be enjoying the music but didn't seem to "get" it. They laughed when the trumpet and trombone players used the "growling" style that had been so popular in New York City. After the intermission, Ellington had the band play more familiar, popular music to please the audience. The critics complained, thinking that he was taking a step down.

A CHANGE OF STYLE

Ellington started to experiment with longer forms than three-minute dance tunes and developed different styles of telling his musical stories. The critics often reacted badly. For example, in 1935, he wrote a longer piece called *Reminiscing in Tempo*, composed while he was still grieving over his mother's death. It was thirteen minutes long, contained no solos, and offered only two simple themes. In other words, it was quite unlike Ellington's previous hits.

Many critics slammed the song. It was "arty and pretentious," sterile, and "not real jazz." Another thought it had promise that it never fulfilled. British journalist Spike Hughes went so far as to call it "a long, rambling monstrosity that is as dull as it is pretentious and meaningless." The *New Yorker*'s reviewer tried to be upbeat, describing it as "unusual and interesting." Horace van Norman, writing for a magazine called the *American Music Lover*, included some praise in his review, such as "there are ... passages which are plainly more eloquent than anything he has written. [*Reminiscing in Tempo* is a] work of incalculable importance, and not to be judged on one or two hearings." Ellington's record company tried to capitalize on the controversy by releasing a flyer that said, "Whatever your musical opinion of this latest work in the modern idiom created by Duke Ellington—trailblazer in the new music—it will not be indifferent!"

But there was one problem: Ellington himself was not at all indifferent to the song. It was one of his most personal compositions. He wrote out every note, including the solo passages, and for once he did not allow his musicians to deviate from what was on the page. Although he never commented on the piece's bad reviews, he must have been insulted. He didn't write another long piece until 1943.

BLACK, BROWN, AND BEIGE

That next work was significant before it was ever played. In 1943, Ellington and the orchestra were asked to play at Carnegie Hall. This was a huge milestone in Ellington's career. In the 1920s and 1930s, only "serious," classical musicians were booked in concert halls. Not only was Ellington a jazz musician, but he was an African-American composer. This was a historic event; Ellington had the chance to present original music in one of the country's most prestigious and well-known venues. He took the opportunity to premiere a new work called Black, Brown, and Beige. Allegedly, it was part of an opera about black history that he intended to write.

As presented that first night, Black, Brown, and Beige was an example of program music. Program music is defined as music that is about or describes something in the real world. This forty-five minute piece was Ellington's attempt to paint a musical portrait of the black experience in America. It was supposed to express various aspects of African-American life, including work, church, emancipation, and civil rights. The music in the first segment was supposed to suggest the lives of African slaves in America. The second part was meant to suggest the participation of African-American soldiers in American wars. The third and final section

From Kentucky Club to Carnegie Hall

-the first of two pages-

JAM SESSIONS OFTEN GIVE BIRTH TO NEW TUNES. ELLINGTON ARRANGEMENTS ARE TRICKY, WRITTEN TO SUIT THE SPECIAL TALENT OF HIS MUSICIANS

Duke Ellington celebrates 20 years
of jazz at the mecca of all musicians

The top man in Negro music climbed on the bandwagon when he and his band played a hot spot called the Kentucky Club. That was twenty years ago, in New York City's Harlem. This year, Duke Ellington made another debut—at Carnegie Hall, goal of the great in music. With him were most of the men who had been with his Famous Orchestra since the early thirties; and the music they played was neither highbrow nor lowdown. The audience heard the same old hot-licks arrangements of Ellington's unique style, the music that has made him famous as a master of the jazz idiom.

Piano lessons bored Ellington when he was six years old. He never learned to play conventionally, but he was only a youngster when his flare for improvisations reaped attention and landed him a job in a Washington theatre. In 1923, he came to New York with the four musicians who formed the nucleus of the orchestra he has today. After a year of miscellaneous night club engagements, he opened at the Kentucky Club in Harlem. From then on, Duke's band was on the long stretch. One by one, his compositions hit the jackpot—*Mood Indigo, Sophisticated Lady, Ebony Rhapsody, Solitude, Caravan, Stormy Weather.* He played the Cotton Club, also in Harlem, in 1927, where he had a national broadcasting hook-up. His versatility kept him occupied. He has done movie shorts (*Black and Tan Fantasy*), vaudeville (with Maurice Chevalier), two European tours which made his music as popular abroad as Mickey Mouse.

Ellington calls his work Negro Music, avoids the terms "jazz" or "swing." "It's still hot, but more subtle," he says. "Whatever it is, it's sure to be original." His fans are inclined to agree.

IN HOLLYWOOD, Duke presented "Ebony Rhapsody," for *Murder at the Vanities.* First among the current vogue of jazz versions of classical music, it was based on the "Hungarian Rhapsody."

This article highlighted the first twenty years of Duke Ellington's career as he prepared to play Carnegie Hall in 1943.

was composed to be a hopeful view of the twentieth century and the idea of integration instead of segregation.

It was not what his fans or critics were expecting to hear. The piece and its performance received mixed reviews. Some music critics said the different parts of the composition didn't come together. Others scoffed at the idea that jazz music could be serious—perhaps thinking that jazz was only for dancing and light entertainment. The classical critics complained that the writing was too informal. There may even have been a touch of racism in the negative reviews because African Americans were playing at Carnegie Hall.

More specifically, the writer Paul Bowles, reviewing for the New York Herald Tribune, criticized Black, Brown, and Beige for being played out of tempo and with no regular beat. He said, "If there is no regular beat there can be no syncopation, and thus no tension, no jazz." Even worse, he called it "a gaudy potpourri of tutti dance passages and solo virtuoso work." John Briggs at the New York Post complained that "Mr. Ellington had set for himself a lofty goal, and with the best intentions did not achieve it." Douglas Wyatt at the Daily News sniped that "such a form of composition is entirely out of Mr. Ellington's ken."

On the other hand, some of the jazz magazines published positive reviews. One critic called it "the elevation of jazz to an orchestral art." The critic for Billboard magazine raved that it was "the first jazz symphony of its time and will point the way to a whole school of jazz literature for the concert stage." To this day, critics disagree about whether Black, Brown, and Beige is any good. Some think it was one of the best works Duke Ellington ever composed, while others say it was an interesting experiment.

Ellington's reaction to these critiques, according to his family, was to stop creating more ambitious, personal works. His sister Ruth observed that the critical response caused him to withdraw and become "very quiet." His son Mercer reported that Ellington

Duke Ellington leads the musicians in performing one of his Sacred Concerts in Coventry, England, in 1966.

stopped writing these large-scale works because "he'd been down that road once, and didn't plan to go there again."

The first night Ellington played *Black, Brown, and Beige*, First Lady Eleanor Roosevelt was in the audience, and the concert was a black-tie affair. His appearance at Carnegie Hall and his performance were that momentous. The piece was never played in its entirety again, though, and was never recorded. Some of its components, however, made a second appearance about twenty years later.

THE SACRED CONCERTS

In 1965, Ellington was offered a commission from an unusual source. The dean of San Francisco's Grace Cathedral asked him to perform a concert of sacred music at the building's consecration. Ellington had long been a man of faith, stretching back to his childhood when he attended two church services a week. He had become more religious over the years, especially following the death of his mother. He studied the Bible and prayed daily. He took this challenge as an opportunity to praise God and celebrate his faith.

The *Concert of Sacred Music*, as it was called, featured the Duke Ellington Orchestra; two choirs, including the Grace Cathedral Choir; two singers; and even a tap dancer, who performed to a song called "David Danced before the Lord with All His Might." Much of the material was adapted from Ellington's earlier works, especially those based on traditional African-American spirituals. He incorporated the songs "New World A-Comin'" and "Come Sunday" from *Black, Brown, and Beige* and "Heritage" from his stage show *My People*. Ellington played "New World A-Comin'" himself, as a piano solo, during the show.

Ellington approached and created this concert with seriousness and sincerity. The San Francisco press gave the show favorable reviews. However, when he played it a second time in New York's Fifth Avenue Presbyterian Church, the reception was not

Duke Ellington signs autographs for some female admirers in 1946.

TRAINS

Duke Ellington had an **affinity** for trains. As a touring musician, he traveled often by train, and because he was on the road so much, he wrote a lot of music while traveling. The train gave him much-needed privacy, and the sound of a train's wheels on the tracks gave him peace. He even loved the blast of the whistle. It was inevitable that the sounds of life on the rails would make its way into his music.

The rhythms in his piece *Reminiscing in Tempo*, for example, were "all caught up in the rhythm and motion of the train dashing through the South." He also wrote other train-related songs, including "Choo-Choo," "Happy-Go-Lucky Local," and "Track 360."

His tune "Daybreak Express" may be his most famous railroad song of all. In it, the band reproduces the sounds of high-speed train travel using ordinary instruments. They create the picture of the train sliding out of the station, gradually getting faster, and whizzing down the track; the train whistle blows as the engine speeds up, then the train (and the music) come to a slow stop as a bell sounds. Cootie Williams replicated the sound of the brakes with his trumpet.

as enthusiastic. Some people, especially members of the clergy, were horrified by its very existence. Some said the music was neither jazz nor classical. Some said jazz could not be religious music and should not be played in church, while others admitted and appreciated that it formed a "bridge" between religion and daily life.

Other critics said the music and words were overly simplified. One even said that it was "commonplace" and "embarrassing."

Alan Rich, writing for the New York Herald Tribune, called it "vintage Ellington ... properly elemental, sometimes brutal, never less than compelling." John Wilson, in the New York Times, said, "Altogether, there was less of the true Ellington stamp on this concert than one would have hoped for." Maybe the best review published after the first New York show was in Ebony magazine: "A type of music once disdained as being only fit for bars and bordellos was being performed in a sacred concert by a man who had helped earn for it the greatest respect."

Many religious leaders were among those who disapproved of the Concert of Sacred Music. Even in his hometown of Washington, DC, the leaders of more than 150 local churches voted not to endorse the concert when it was presented at the District's Constitution Hall.

Duke Ellington had the last laugh, though. He won a Grammy Award for one of the concert's featured original pieces, "In the Beginning, God." When public television aired two documentaries based on the concert's rehearsals and performance, one of them won an Emmy Award.

Ellington wrote two more Sacred Concerts after the first. One of his many honorary degrees came from the Christian Theological Seminary in Indianapolis, Indiana, "for his contributions to the field of sacred music."

Other than a few exceptions, Duke Ellington tried not to pay attention to the critics. His opinion was that criticism "stunk up the place." He also preferred to keep moving forward with his music rather than looking back. And despite anything any critic ever said about him, he was in demand for most of his fifty-year career. He played countless shows all over the United States, as well as more than twenty thousand performances in Europe, Latin America, the Middle East, and Asia.

HONORS AND ACCOLADES

Duke Ellington was recognized frequently for his achievements both during and after his long lifetime. Some of those recognitions were minor but flattering. For example, after his groundbreaking, career-reviving performance at the Newport Jazz Festival in 1956, he was featured on the cover of *Time* magazine.

During the 1960s and 1970s alone, he received the keys to eighteen different cities and honorary degrees from almost twenty colleges and universities. The first was from Washington University in St. Louis, where he was awarded an honorary doctorate of music. The second was from Yale University, the school's first honorary degree to be conferred upon a jazz musician. The crowd gave Ellington a standing ovation when he went up onstage to receive it. He got several more from schools including Brown, Columbia, and Howard Universities. When the University of Wisconsin–Madison invited him to receive an honorary degree, they also asked him to present a week of master classes. He ended the week with a concert at the student union.

Ellington received awards from three presidents, including Dwight D. Eisenhower, who gave him the President's Award for Special Merit. President Lyndon B. Johnson gave him the President's Gold Medal and appointed him to the National Council of the Arts. President Richard M. Nixon presented him with the Presidential Medal of Freedom in 1969.

Duke Ellington holding two of the Grammy Awards he won in 1968.

Not to be outdone, France presented him with the Legion of Honor award. Ethiopia gave him the Emperor's Star. In both cases, those were the highest honors the countries could bestow. Ellington was buried wearing the Legion of Honor and the Presidential Medal of Freedom.

Two African nations, Togo and Chad, issued stamps in his honor. (The United States Postal Service created a commemorative stamp with his image on it in 1986. They do not depict living people on their stamps.) In response, Ellington composed the *Togo Brava Suite* and premiered it at the 1971 Newport Jazz Festival.

In 1971, the Royal Swedish Academy of Music honored Ellington by inducting him as the first non-classical member in its two-hundred-year history.

The National Association for the Advancement of Colored People, who once offered Ellington a scholarship to the Pratt Institute, gave him the Spingarn Medal in 1959 for outstanding achievement by an African American.

Then there were the Grammy Awards, given out by the National Academy of Recording Arts and Sciences. The Grammys are the recording industry's most prestigious awards. They are peer honors, voted on by artists and technical professionals and given to their colleagues for artistic or technical achievement, not for sales or chart positions. Ellington received eleven individual Grammy Awards in categories including Best Jazz Instrumental Performance, Big Band, and Best Jazz Performance by a Big Band.

He also won Best Instrumental Jazz Performance by a Large Group or Soloist with Large Group three times, Best Original Jazz Composition once, Best Instrumental Composition, Best Soundtrack Album - Background Score from a Motion Picture or Television, and simply Best Performance by an Orchestra. His music was also honored when singer Ella Fitzgerald won one of her fourteen Grammys for her album *Ella Fitzgerald Sings the Duke Ellington Song Book*. Finally, the academy also honored him with a Lifetime Achievement Award in 1966.

Ellington was nominated for both an Oscar and a Primetime Emmy Award, but he did not win either. He was one of the first ten people to be inducted into the Songwriters' Hall of Fame in 1971.

One award Ellington did not receive in his lifetime was the Pulitzer Prize. He was nominated in 1965 but did not win. The three-person jury was outraged that their unanimous recommendation for him to receive the award was rejected. They accused the advisory board of racism, and two of the jury members resigned over the incident. As it turns out, he didn't win because he was being nominated for four decades of work, while the advisory board wanted to stick to the rules of the award being given for a particular piece of music. Ellington was not as bothered by not winning as he was by the public controversy that resulted. He was horrified that the story was reported in the papers. However, when asked for his feelings about the situation, he responded professionally: "I feel very lucky to have been mentioned at all for such an honor," he said. "Fate is being too kind to me. Fate doesn't want me to be too famous too young."

Luck is a theme that runs throughout Duke Ellington's long life and career. He talked of getting lucky breaks and of being lucky enough to meet certain people. Although he was superstitious about most things, he considered thirteen to be his lucky number. But his success, of course, did not come just from luck. It came from his unique style and his willingness to stick to what he did best, even when the critics and the public were not always on his side.

CHAPTER SIX

A LASTING LEGACY

Throughout his career, Duke Ellington and his music were tremendously influential. In the 1920s, he was one of the most popular and prolific musicians in New York City. He played a huge role in the emergence of the Harlem Renaissance movement. He became famous nationwide when his concerts at the Cotton Club were broadcast over the radio. He was also a showman, using lighting and screens to create drama when he and his orchestra performed. His style of composition brought fame to his musicians when he featured them in solos that played to their strengths. His personal style and image also played a role in his fame. Whether he liked it or not, he was strongly associated with jazz music, which was hugely popular throughout the decade.

In the 1930s, the Great Depression had taken over the country. People lost their savings, their jobs, and even their lives. Americans wanted to hear music that could cheer them up. That music was a different form of jazz, called swing. Most of the early famous

Opposite: Ellington's style remained consistent throughout the years.

The marquee at the famed Apollo Theater in Harlem advertises a performance of Duke Ellington's *Nutcracker Suite* in 2014.

swing bands were white. Some of the most popular bandleaders of the swing era were Tommy Dorsey, Glenn Miller, and Benny Goodman. The public didn't realize that these white musicians were building on what African-American musicians had been playing for years. Ellington didn't care much for swing, but he did care that some of these new swing bands were scoring hits by playing and recording some of his songs, like "Solitude" and "In a Sentimental Mood." He allowed his manager, Irving Mills, to promote the band as a swing group. He also continued to compose, and his work from the big-band era stands out from everyone else's. There are three reasons for this: Billy Strayhorn, bassist Jimmie Blanton, and saxophonist Ben Webster. The years that Strayhorn wrote with Ellington, while Blanton and Webster played with the band, are often called the Duke Ellington Orchestra's greatest era.

DECLINE AND REVIVAL

As the 1940s wore on and jazz music (including swing and big band) began to fade from popularity, Ellington turned his talents to two different styles of music. First, he wrote *Jump for Joy*, his first full-length stage show. It was an all-black revue, and its stars included his own singer Ivie Anderson and famous black actress Dorothy Dandridge. Poet Langston Hughes, a fellow player in the Harlem Renaissance, contributed a sketch. *Jump for Joy* got decent reviews, but its importance lay mostly in the fact that it portrayed African Americans with dignity. In 1943, Duke premiered his piece *Black, Brown, and Beige* at Carnegie Hall (see Chapter Five for more about this composition). By the end of World War II, singers were becoming more popular than bands. Television took over as people's main source of entertainment. Members of the Duke Ellington Orchestra couldn't even travel by train anymore, since the trains were needed to transport the troops.

JUMP FOR JOY

From the American Revue Theatre Production "JUMP FOR JOY"

Lyric by
PAUL WEBSTER
and **SID KULLER**

Music by
DUKE ELLINGTON

We're so fed up with the South-land that way down South in the Mouth-land. For all these years we've been bored to tears with the blues ——— Those south-ern songs are get-ting tired.— they're sweet, beat and un - in - spired.— It's

SH 2228-3

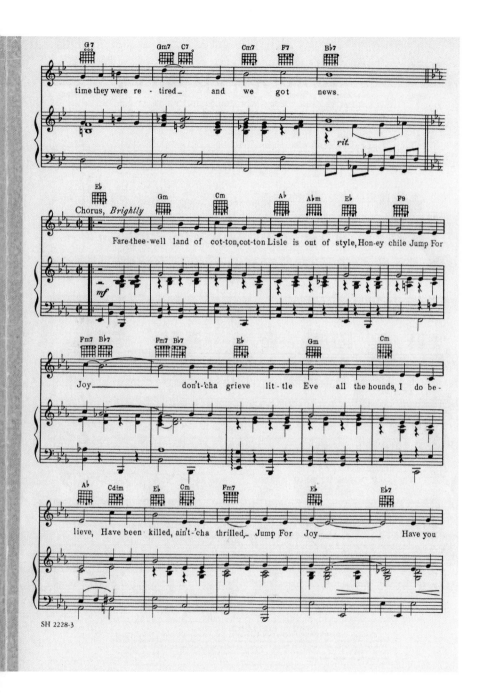

Sheet music for "Jump for Joy," a 1941 musical revue

DUKE AND CIVIL RIGHTS

While Duke Ellington did not engage actively in the civil rights movement by participating in protests, this doesn't mean that he didn't show his support in other ways. He made a practice of giving generously to charities that fought against racial prejudice. He and his orchestra also performed at many benefits for the NAACP, an important organization that fights for racial equality.

Even after the performance of *Black, Brown, and Beige*, Ellington was often criticized by those in the civil rights movement for not fighting enough against segregation and racial prejudice. In response, he wrote: "I am not the sort who makes speeches—or even statements of this kind. Instead, as always, I stand on what I have done and will continue to do."

But not everyone thought that Ellington wasn't a friend to the civil rights movement. In the early 1960s, he met Dr. Martin Luther King Jr. for the first time. According to the civil rights activist Marion Logan, they ran up to one another and embraced "like old friends." Later that day, King presented Ellington with a special award for helping make America better through music.

Throughout the 1950s, Ellington continued to compose, and the band continued to play, but many of their peers were no longer around. One exception was Benny Goodman, and the Duke Ellington Orchestra suffered a great loss when Cootie Williams quit them to join Goodman's group. Barney Bigard left the band because he was tired of traveling and wanted to settle down with his new wife. Juan Tizol also quit to join another band. Tricky Sam Nanton died.

There was also a new musical sound taking over: rock and roll. Nothing could be further from jazz, swing, or big-band music. Teenagers were becoming a driving force in the music industry because of it, and Ellington's records were not selling. For a time, it seemed like the Duke Ellington Orchestra had reached the end of the line.

Then came the Newport Jazz Festival in 1956. Although Ellington and his orchestra were not slated to be the stars of the show, they changed their own history that night. As discussed in Chapter Two, they won over the crowd with their remake of "Diminuendo and Crescendo in Blue," featuring a long, powerful solo by Paul Gonsalves. By the end of the performance, Duke Ellington was once again a force to be reckoned with in the music industry. People began buying his records again and never stopped. He himself would describe the festival as the rebirth of his career.

In the 1960s, the Duke Ellington Orchestra spent a lot of time overseas. They played in Europe, as always, but they also performed in countries where jazz was new. Ellington served as an unofficial ambassador of jazz in India, Japan, Russia, and the countries of Latin America and Eastern Europe. He closed out the decade with his Sacred Concerts.

DUKE'S LEGACY

The great Duke Ellington was a musical **pioneer**. He wrote music like nobody else, and that music has endured. Jazz groups and symphony orchestras still play his songs today, pop singers and opera singers sing them, and musical scholars study them. Sometimes, performing his music can be difficult because Ellington didn't always write everything down. But Mercer Ellington donated his father's papers, scores, and other **memorabilia** to the Smithsonian, the world's largest museum and research complex, which helped to clarify some of the composer's musical intentions.

Mercer, of course, continued to lead the Duke Ellington Orchestra for two decades after his father passed away. After Mercer died, his son Paul took over, although he had never known his famous grandfather. The Duke Ellington Orchestra still exists and still tours today, although it is now managed by an entertainment company.

From 1981 to 1983, Mercer also served as the musical director and conductor of *Sophisticated Ladies*, a Broadway revue of his father's music (named after the Duke's famous song "Sophisticated Lady") starring Gregory Hines. The show recreated Ellington's big-band sound and featured all of his most famous numbers, including "It Don't Mean a Thing (If It Ain't Got That Swing)," "Take the 'A' Train," "Satin Doll," and "In a Sentimental Mood."

Musicians who list Duke Ellington and his music as having a strong influence on their careers include double bassist, composer, and bandleader Charles Mingus; composer, bandleader, and pianist Sun Ra (also known as Herman "Sonny" Blount); trumpet player and composer Lester Bowie; jazz pianist and composer Thelonius Monk; and modern composer and trumpeter Wynton Marsalis.

Charles (Charlie) Mingus not only grew up listening to the music of Duke Ellington on the radio, he actually played with the Duke Ellington Orchestra for a brief time in the 1950s. He holds the distinction of being one of the few musicians ever to

Gregory Hines starred in *Sophisticated Ladies*, a musical revue based on Duke Ellington's music, on Broadway in 1981.

be fired by Ellington. He claims it was the result of him picking a fight with Juan Tizol. Still, Ellington and Mingus later recorded a trio album called *Money Jungle* along with drummer Max Roach.

Although he is mostly associated with old-school jazz, Ellington's work had a profound effect on some of the modern era's most avant-garde jazz composers. Keyboardist and composer Sun Ra always said that he was influenced by Ellington's work. He even recorded an album called *Duke Ellington's Sound of Space*, which presented his interpretation of Ellington's music. Trumpet player Lester Bowie was given the nickname "the new Cootie Williams" because he used mutes in the "wah-wah" style that the Duke Ellington Orchestra musician popularized in the 1920s and 1930s. As for Thelonius Monk, his reinterpretations of Ellington's music got the attention of the man himself when Ellington overheard Ray Nance playing Monk's album *Thelonius Monk Plays the Music of Duke Ellington*.

Trumpeter, bandleader, and composer Miles Davis, another of the twentieth century's most influential musicians, often expressed his admiration for Ellington's style, work, and contributions to the music world. Reportedly, Davis's mother played Ellington's records when Miles was growing up. Robert G. O'Meally, founder of the Center for Jazz Studies at Columbia University reports that Davis once said, "[A]s a jazz musician, he and all his brothers and sisters in the music [industry] should bow down every day and thank Duke Ellington for being part of this world."

WYNTON MARSALIS

Wynton Marsalis would probably agree with Davis's proclamation. He has done more than any other musician of this generation to ensure Duke Ellington's **legacy**, as well as to preserve the art of jazz. He has called Ellington his hero, although he didn't start listening to Ellington's music until he was in his teens. "That's when I discovered for the first time that jazz could be so sophisticated,"

Marsalis has said. "Duke's work was an entirely original blend of New Orleans jazz, blues, spirituals, American folk music, and various European forms—a complex brew that was uniquely itself." He was also inspired by Ellington's work ethic. Ellington was still touring and playing every day and writing every night into his seventies. Marsalis has also said, "From Ellington I learned the value of nonstop learning—I still take the occasional lesson—of practicing, of being a responsible and responsive part of a group, of having a good time, of embracing difficult things."

In 1987, Marsalis co-founded a jazz program at Lincoln Center in New York City—called Jazz at Lincoln Center. The program has highlighted Ellington's music frequently. The most recent events included a Duke Ellington Festival in 2013, a "Modern Ellington" concert performed in honor of his birthday in 2014, and the center's April 2015 gala, which was called "The World of Duke Ellington" and promised to celebrate "the indomitable spirit of swing and legacy of Duke Ellington, the most influential figure in American music."

UNEXPECTED INFLUENCES

Sometimes Ellington's work influenced other, unexpected artists. Jimi Hendrix was one of the great rock-and-roll guitarists of the 1960s, famous for his psychedelic style on the electric guitar. When he heard "East St. Louis Toodle-Oo," he liked Bubber Miley's solo so much that he tried to duplicate its sound by using a "wah-wah" pedal to alter the sound of his guitar. In the 1970s, Steely Dan was a jazz-rock group that also blended funk, R&B, and pop into their easy-listening sound. They recorded their own arrangement of "East St. Louis Toodle-Oo." In 2012, punk-pop pianist Joe Jackson released a Duke Ellington tribute album, titled *The Duke*. Musical guests who worked with him on the album include punk rocker Iggy Pop, soul singer Sharon Jones, jazz violinist Regina Carter, drummer Questlove of the Roots, award-winning jazz bassist

Wynton Marsalis, shown here conducting the Lincoln Center Jazz Orchestra, has been instrumental in keeping Duke Ellington's legacy alive.

Christian McBride, and electric guitarist Steve Vai. The songs covered on the album included "Caravan," "Mood Indigo," "Satin Doll," "The Mooche," "Black and Tan Fantasy," and "It Don't Mean A Thing (If It Ain't Got That Swing)."

Countless musicians, singers, and bands have released tribute albums of themselves playing or singing Ellington's music. Ella Fitzgerald was one of the most famous of these artists. On her album *Ella Fitzgerald Sings the Duke Ellington Song Book*, she was actually accompanied by Ellington and some of his orchestra members, including Billy Strayhorn, Paul Gonsalves, Ben Webster, Johnny Hodges, Russell Procope, Harry Carney, and Ray Nance. Fitzgerald's performance on this album won her one of her fourteen Grammy Awards. She recorded with Ellington three more times, on the albums *Ella and Duke at the Cote D'Azur, The Stockholm Concert,* and *Ella at Duke's Place.*

Harry Connick Jr., a native of New Orleans, introduced a whole new generation to Ellington's music in 1989, when he performed on the soundtrack to the movie *When Harry Met Sally.* His rendition of "Don't Get Around Much Anymore" featured prominently in the film. The same year, his album *Twenty* included the Ellington song "Do Nothin' Till You Hear From Me," and Connick offered his interpretation of "Caravan" on his 1992 album *Twenty-Five.* He has also played at the Duke Ellington Jazz Festival.

Ellington's tunes have been used on many television shows, including The *Sopranos, Boardwalk Empire*, and *Breaking Bad.* They've shown up in more than one hundred movies, including *Ocean's Eleven* (the 2001 version) and its sequel *Ocean's Thirteen, The Notebook, Divine Secrets of the Ya-Ya Sisterhood, The Matrix, Saving Private Ryan,* and *The Big Lebowski.*

Renowned jazz singer Ella Fitzgerald and Duke Ellington posed for photos to help publicize the release of *Ella Sings the Duke Ellington Song Book*.

POSTHUMOUS TRIBUTES

Ellington was memorialized in a hit song by African-American pianist, songwriter, and singer Stevie Wonder in 1977. Wonder, who has also earned numerous hit records and Grammy Awards over his own long career, wrote his hit "Sir Duke" as a tribute to Ellington. He also wanted the song to be a reminder of many of the other influential musicians who should be remembered, such as Count Basie, Louis Armstrong, and Ella Fitzgerald.

The first two verses of the song state:

Music is a world within itself
With a language we all understand
With an equal opportunity
For all to sing, dance, and clap their hands
But just because a record has a groove
Don't make it in the groove
But you can tell right away at letter A
When the people start to move
Music knows it is and always will
Be one of the things that life just won't quit
But here are some of music's pioneers
That time will not allow us to forget
For there's Basie, Miller, Satchmo
And the king of all Sir Duke
And with a voice like Ella's ringing out
There's no way the band can lose

The song went to number one on both the R&B and pop charts during the spring of 1977 and still receives heavy rotation on oldies stations.

Shortly after Ellington died, singer, pianist, and jazz interpreter Bobby Short formed the Duke Ellington Memorial Fund. His mission was to raise enough money to have a statue of Ellington

This statue of Duke Ellington and his piano stands at the "gateway to Harlem" in New York City.

designed, produced, and installed in New York's Central Park. It took eighteen years to raise the money, but when the statue was dedicated, three New York City mayors—Edward I. Koch, David N. Dinkins, and Rudolph W. Giuliani—made speeches. Bobby Short and trumpeter Wynton Marsalis, who established the Jazz at Lincoln Center program, both performed. American artist Robert Graham sculpted the bronze statue. It stands 30 feet tall (9.1 meters tall) on three columns. Three female figures representing the muses, with their arms raised, each stand on top of a column, which together support a circular platform. An 8-foot-high (2.4-meter-high) figure of Duke Ellington standing beside a piano tops the platform. The interior of the platform is gilded in gold. The statue stands at "the gateway to Harlem," the junction of Fifth Avenue and 110th Street in New York City.

Another lasting tribute to Duke Ellington is the Duke Ellington School of the Arts, established in 1974 in his hometown of Washington, DC. The school's mission statement reads: "Starting young, learning in a disciplined yet improvisational manner, flourishing in a tough world, developing a lifelong network of fruitful relationships—all these accomplishments are represented in the life of the composer, bandleader, and Washington, DC native, Edward Kennedy 'Duke' Ellington. His are the qualities we have worked to instill in graduates since the Duke Ellington School of the Arts was founded nearly forty years ago." Famous alumni of the school include comedian Dave Chappelle, R&B singer Johnny Gill, and opera singer Denyce Graves. The center hosts an annual Duke Ellington birthday celebration, which is a performance staged on the Sunday closest to Ellington's birthday, April 29.

A minor but touching tribute is the Duke Ellington Ballroom at Northern Illinois University. NIU is where Ellington played his final full concert on March 20, 1974. As a professional and

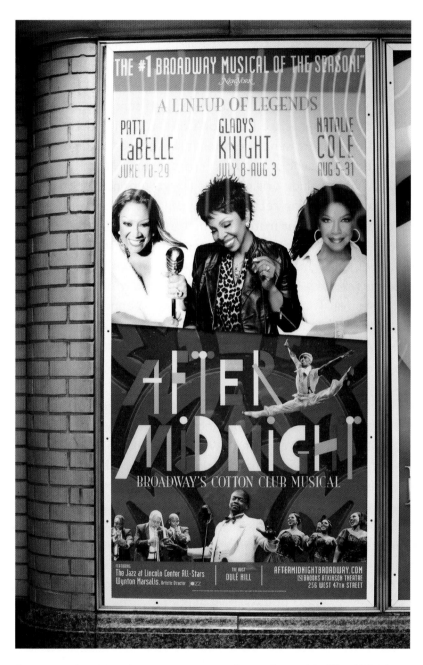

A poster advertising the various singers who performed in *After Midnight* on Broadway in 2014

dedicated musician, Ellington felt that "the show must go on" even though he was very sick and in obvious pain. He died of cancer just two months later.

The annual Essentially Ellington High School Jazz Band Competition and Festival encourages high school musicians to perform and appreciate Ellington's music. During the year, the festival organizers send membership packages to high school and secondary school band directors around North America. The packages include original Duke Ellington transcription charts, their corresponding recordings by the Jazz at Lincoln Center Orchestra, and other materials. The bands record their versions of the songs, and the audition recordings are sent to Lincoln Center. A judging panel picks the top fifteen bands through a blind screening process. Each finalist band flies to New York to compete in the festival. The final three bands play at a concert along with Wynton Marsalis and the Jazz at Lincoln Center Orchestra. After the concert, awards for the top three bands are announced. This is yet another way that Wynton Marsalis is helping to keep Duke Ellington's legacy alive.

Recently, the story of Duke Ellington and his years at the Cotton Club was told through another Broadway musical called *After Midnight*. An orchestra of world-class musicians, the Jazz at Lincoln Center All-Stars, hand-picked by Wynton Marsalis, played the music of Duke Ellington, Harold Arlen, Cab Calloway, and others. The setting for the show was Harlem, mostly inside a nightclub, and the words spoken by the host were taken from poems by Harlem Renaissance author Langston Hughes. Choreographer Warren Carlyle won a Tony Award for the dance moves he created. Eleven of Ellington's songs featured prominently in the revue: "Daybreak Express," "Braggin' in Brass," "East St. Louis Toodle-Oo," "The Skrontch," "Creole Love Call," "The Mooche," "The Gal From

Joe's," "Black and Tan Fantasy," "Tap Mathematician," "It Don't Mean a Thing (If It Ain't Got That Swing)," "Cotton Club Stomp," and "Rockin' in Rhythm." Ellington did not compose the other sixteen songs in the musical, but he had created orchestrations for them when he played them with the Washingtonians. The musical director chose to use those orchestrations. Originally starring television actor Dulé Hill and pop singer Fantasia, the show was a huge hit with audiences. Thirty years after his death, Duke Ellington's music once again prompted thunderous applause on a New York City stage.

Throughout his life, Duke Ellington's music **transcended** boundaries and brought different styles of music and different groups of people together. But this didn't end after his death. Even today, Ellington's treasure trove of music renews itself through every generation of fans and music-lovers. His legacy continues to live on and will endure for generations to come.

CHRONOLOGY

1899 Born to James Edward Ellington and Daisy Kennedy Ellington.

1913 Attends Armstrong High School and studies art.

1914 Job at Poodle Dog Café, where he composes his first song.

1915 Sister Ruth is born.

1917–1919 Plays music in cafes and clubs in Washington, DC.

1917 Forms his first group, (The) Duke's Serenaders.

1918 Marries his high school girlfriend, Edna Thompson.

1919 Becomes a father when Mercer Kennedy Ellington is born.

1923 Moves to New York, encouraged by Fats Waller.

1924 Releases his first record with the Washingtonians.

1926 Records "East St. Louis Toodle-Oo".

1927 Starts new position as the house band at Harlem's Cotton Club.

1932–1942 Golden age for the band.

1933 The Duke Ellington Orchestra tours three countries in Europe.

1935 Records *Reminiscing in Tempo*.

1940 Participates in the civil rights movement.

1941 Writes score for *Jump for Joy*.

1943 Performs *Black, Brown, and Beige* at Carnegie Hall.

1954 Featured on the cover of *Time* magazine.

1965 Explores spiritual themes through the *Concert of Sacred Music*.

1965 Nominated for the Pulitzer Prize.

1969 Awarded the Presidential Medal of Freedom by Richard Nixon.

1971 Inducted into the Royal Swedish Academy of Music.

1973 Publishes his autobiography, titled *Music is My Mistress*.

1974 Passes away after suffering from lung cancer and pneumonia.

1986 Posthumously honored by the United States Postal Service with a commemorative stamp bearing his image.

ELLINGTON'S MOST IMPORTANT WORKS

SHORTER WORKS

"Black and Tan Fantasy" (1927)
"Creole Love Call" (1927)
"East St. Louis Toodle-Oo" (1927)
"Mood Indigo" (1931)
"Rockin' in Rhythm" (1931)
"It Don't Mean a Thing (If It Ain't Got That Swing)" (1932)
"Sophisticated Lady" (1933)
"Drop Me Off at Harlem" (1933)
"Solitude" (1934)
"In a Sentimental Mood" (1935)
"Caravan" (1937)
"Diminuendo and Crescendo in Blue" (1938)
"Boy Meets Horn" (1938)
"I Let a Song Go Out of My Heart" (1938)
"Prelude to a Kiss" (1938)
"Concerto for Cootie" (1939)
"I Got It Bad and That Ain't Good" (1941)
"Satin Doll" (1953)

LONGER WORKS

Creole Rhapsody (1931)
Reminiscing in Tempo (1935)
Jump for Joy (1941)
Black, Brown, and Beige (1945)
The Deep South Suite (1946)
The Liberian Suite (1947)
The Tattooed Bride (1948)
Harlem (1950)
Night Creature (1955)
Newport Jazz Festival Suite (1956)
My People (1963)
The Far East Suite (1964)
Concert of Sacred Music (1965)
Second Sacred Concert (1968)
Third Sacred Concert (1974)

GLOSSARY

activist Someone who demonstrates direct, vigorous action in support of or opposition to one side of a controversial issue.

coddle To treat with extreme or excessive care or kindness.

condolence An expression of sympathy and sadness when someone is suffering because of the death of a family member, a friend, etc.

encompass To include (something) as a part.

eulogy A speech that praises someone who has died.

evoke To bring (a memory, feeling, image, etc.) into the mind.

gig A job usually for a specified time; especially an entertainer's engagement.

improvisation Speaking or performing without preparation.

infidelity Marital unfaithfulness.

legacy Something that is handed down from someone in the past.

light-skinned Especially with regards to a nonwhite person, having pale or relatively pale skin.

lucrative Producing money or wealth.

lynching To put to death (as by hanging) by mob action, without legal sanction.

memorabilia Things that are remarkable and worthy of remembrance, or things that stir recollection or are valued or collected for their association with a particular field or interest.

middle class The social class that is between the upper class and the lower class and that includes mainly business and professional people, government officials, and skilled workers.

obscurity The state of being unknown or forgotten.

pioneer A person who helps create or develop new ideas, methods, etc.

reminiscing Talking, thinking, or writing about things that happened in the past.

revue A theatrical production consisting typically of brief, loosely connected, often satirical skits, songs, and dances.

segregated Maintaining divided facilities for members of different groups or races.

splurge To spend more money than usual on something.

synonymous Describing something that is equivalent or very similar to something else.

synthesized To make something new by combining different things.

transcend To rise above or go beyond the normal limits of something.

unfaithful Having an intimate relationship with someone who is not your wife, husband, or partner.

FURTHER INFORMATION

BOOKS

Collier, James Lincoln. *Duke Ellington*. Oxford, UK: Oxford University Press, 1987.

Dance, Stanley. *The World of Duke Ellington*. New York, NY: Da Capo Press, 2000.

Ellington, Duke. *Music is My Mistress*. New York, NY: Da Capo Press, 1973.

Ellington, Mercer, and Stanley Dance. *Duke Ellington In Person: An Intimate Memoir*. New York, NY: Da Capo Press, 1979.

Hasse, John Edward, and Wynton Marsalis. *Beyond Category: The Life and Genius of Duke Ellington*. New York, NY: Da Capo Press, 1995.

Tucker, Mark, ed. *The Duke Ellington Reader*. Oxford, UK: Oxford University Press, 1993.

WEBSITES

Duke Ellington Biography
www.biography.com/people/duke-ellington-9286338
Biography.com offers a concise, informative summary of Duke Ellington's life.

The Duke Ellington Society
www.thedukeellingtonsociety.org/dukeellington/dukebio.asp
Founded in 1959, the Duke Ellington Society pays tribute to Ellington and his longtime collaborator, Billy Strayhorn. Their website includes biographical information and suggested reading and listening lists.

Jazz: Duke Ellington
www.pbs.org/jazz/biography/artist_id_ellington_duke.htm
The companion website for Ken Burns's landmark documentary *Jazz* features a Duke Ellington section, complete with numerous audio samples.

The Official Site of Jazz Legend Duke Ellington
www.dukeellington.com/home.html
This website offers a range of resources on Duke Ellington, including his biography, his discography, and a photo archive, as well as current tour dates for the Duke Ellington Orchestra.

BIBLIOGRAPHY

BOOKS

Biography.com Editors. "Duke Ellington." Accessed September 23, 2015. http://www.biography.com/people/duke-ellington-9286338#related-video-gallery.

Brown, Gene. *Duke Ellington: Jazz Master.* Woodbridge, CT: Blackbirch Press, 2001.

Chambers, Veronica. *The Harlem Renaissance*. Philadelphia, PA: Chelsea House, 1998.

Haskins, Jim. *The Harlem Renaissance*. Brookfield, CT: The Millbrook Press, 1996.

Hillstrom, Kevin. *Defining Moments: The Harlem Renaissance*. Detroit, MI: Omnigraphics, 2008.

Jazz at Lincoln Center. "Duke Ellington." PBS. Accessed September 23, 2015. http://www.pbs.org/jazz/biography/artist_id_ellington_duke.htm.

Koopmans, Andy. *The Harlem Renaissance*. Lucent Library of Black History. Farmington Hills, MI: Thomson-Gale, 2006.

Lawrence, A. H. *Duke Ellington and His World: A Biography*. New York, NY: Routledge, 2001.

Library of Congress. "Duke Ellington." America's Story from America's Library. Accessed September 23, 2015. http://www. americaslibrary.gov/aa/ellington/aa_ellington_subj.html.

Marks, Carole, and Diana Edkins. *The Power of Pride: Stylemakers and Rulebreakers of the Harlem Renaissance.* New York, NY: Crown Publishers, 1999.

"The Official Site of Jazz Legend Duke Ellington." Accessed September 23, 2015. http://www.dukeellington.com/home.html.

Oppenheim, Mike. "The Harlem Renaissance and American Music." All About Jazz, March 3, 2013. Accessed September 23, 2015. http://www.allaboutjazz.com/the-harlem-renaissance-and-american-music-by-mike-oppenheim.php.

Suzanne. "Duke Ellington and the Harlem Renaissance." *The Year of Tony Bennett* (blog), April 28, 2013. Accessed September 23, 2015. http://bloggingtonybennett.com/duke-ellington-and-the-harlem-renaissance.

Teachout, Terry. *Duke: A Life of Duke Ellington.* New York, NY: Gotham Books, 2013.

Tucker, Mark. *Ellington: The Early Years.* Chicago, IL: University of Illinois Press, 1991.

Woog, Adam. *The Importance of Duke Ellington.* San Diego, CA: Lucent Books, 1996.

INDEX

Page numbers in **boldface** are illustrations. Entries in **boldface** are glossary terms.

Rebecca Carey Rohan lives in upstate New York with her two children and three rescued pets. She is the author of *Working with Electricity: Electrical Engineers*, *Great American Thinkers: Thurgood Marshall*, and two other titles in the Artists of the Harlem Renaissance series, *Billie Holiday* and *Langston Hughes*.